BANKING AND BANKING DEVELOPMENTS

THE EXPORT-IMPORT BANK OF THE UNITED STATES

ACTIVITIES, COMPETITIVENESS AND INTERNATIONAL COMPARISONS

BANKING AND BANKING DEVELOPMENTS

Additional books in this series can be found on Nova's website
under the Series tab.

Additional E-books in this series can be found on Nova's website
under the E-book tab.

BANKING AND BANKING DEVELOPMENTS

THE EXPORT-IMPORT BANK OF THE UNITED STATES

ACTIVITIES, COMPETITIVENESS AND INTERNATIONAL COMPARISONS

FRASER M. MULDER
EDITOR

nova publishers
New York

Library of Congress Cataloging-in-Publication Data

ISBN: 978-1-62618-709-2

Published by Nova Science Publishers, Inc. † New York

CONTENTS

PREFACE

The Export-Import Bank of the United States (Ex-Im Bank, EXIM Bank, or the Bank), an independent federal government agency, is the official export credit agency of the United States. It helps finance U.S. exports of manufactured goods and services, with the objective of contributing to the employment of U.S. workers, primarily in circumstances when alternative financing is not available. The Ex-Im Bank also may assist U.S. exporters to meet foreign, officially sponsored, export credit competition. Its main programs are direct loans, loan guarantees, working capital guarantees, and export credit insurance. Ex-Im Bank transactions are backed by the full faith and credit of the U.S. government. This book examines issues related to the Ex-Im Bank that center on the economic rationale for the Bank; the impact of the Bank on the federal budget and U.S. taxpayers; the Bank's support for specific types of business or industries; the current balance between the Bank's advancement of U.S. commercial interests and other U.S. policy goals; and the Bank's organizational structure.

Chapter 1 – The Export-Import Bank of the United States (Ex-Im Bank, EXIM Bank, or the Bank), an independent federal government agency, is the official export credit agency (ECA) of the United States. It helps finance U.S. exports of manufactured goods and services, with the objective of contributing to the employment of U.S. workers, primarily in circumstances when alternative financing is not available. The Ex-Im Bank also may assist U.S. exporters to meet foreign, officially sponsored, export credit competition. Its main programs are direct loans, loan guarantees, working capital guarantees, and export credit insurance. Ex-Im Bank transactions are backed by the full faith and credit of the U.S. government. The Ex-Im Bank is a participant in President Obama's National Export Initiative (NEI), a plan to double exports by 2015 to support 2 million U.S. jobs. The Bank operates under a renewable charter, the Export-Import Bank Act of 1945, as amended. The charter requires that all of the Bank's financing have a reasonable assurance of repayment and directs the Bank to supplement, and to not compete with, private capital.

In light of the international financial crisis, demand for Ex-Im Bank services has grown in recent years. In FY2011, the Bank approved more than 3,700 transactions of credit and insurance support, totaling about $33 billion— the highest level of authorizations in the history of the Bank. The Ex-Im Bank estimated that its credit and insurance activities supported about $41 billion in U.S. exports of goods and services, and were associated with 290,000 U.S. jobs, in FY2011.

The Ex-Im Bank has been "self-sustaining" for appropriations purposes since FY2008. It uses offsetting collections to cover its administrative expenses and program operations. Congress sets an upper limit on the level of the Bank's financial activities as part of the annual appropriations process. For FY2012, Congress appropriated $4 million for the Ex-Im Bank's Office of Inspector General (OIG), and authorized a limit of $58 million on the total amount that the Ex-Im Bank can spend on its credit and insurance programs and a limit of $89.9 million for the Bank's administrative expenses (P.L. 112-74). For FY2013, the President requested an appropriation of $4.4 million for the OIG, a limit of $38 million on the Bank's program activities, and a limit of $103.9 million for the Bank's administrative expenses. Since 1990, the Ex-Im Bank has retuned to the U.S. Treasury $4.9 billion more than it received in appropriations.

The Organization for Economic Cooperation and Development (OECD) "Arrangement on Export Credits" sets forth export credit terms and conditions, including restrictions on tied aid, for the activities of the Ex-Im Bank and the ECAs of foreign countries that are OECD members. Other OECD agreements set forth sector-specific rules, guidelines on environmental procedures, and other terms and conditions.

The 112th Congress has considered several pieces of legislation to renew the Ex-Im Bank's charter, which previously had been extended to May 31, 2012 (P.L. 112-74). Most recently, Congress has passed a bill to extend the Ex-Im Bank's authority through FY2014 (H.R. 2072). Members of Congress may examine issues related to the Ex-Im Bank that center on the economic rationale for the Bank; the impact of the Bank on the federal budget and U.S. taxpayers; the Bank's support for specific types of business or industries; the current balance between the Bank's advancement of U.S. commercial interests and other U.S. policy goals; the competitive position of the Bank compared to foreign ECAs; and the Bank's organizational structure.

Chapter 2 – The Export-Import Bank of the United States (Ex-Im Bank, EXIM Bank, or the Bank), a self-sustaining agency, is the official U.S. export credit agency (ECA). It operates under a renewable charter, the Export-Import Bank Act of 1945 (P.L. 79-173), as amended. Potential issues for Congress in examining the Ex-Im Bank's authority include the following:

- **The economic rationale for the Bank**, including the role of the federal government in export promotion and finance;
- **Specific Bank policies**, such as those relating to content, shipping, economic and environmental impact analysis, and tied aid, including how these policies balance U.S. export and other policy interests;
- **Statutory requirements directing the Ex-Im Bank to support certain types of exports**, such as exports of small businesses and "green" technology, including the tension that such requirements can create between desiring to support specific economic sectors and allowing the Ex-Im Bank flexibility to fulfill its mission to support U.S. exports and jobs; and
- **International developments that may affect the Bank's work**, such as the growing role of emerging economies' ECAs and the sufficiency of the Organization for Economic Cooperation and Development (OECD) Arrangement on Officially Supported Export Credits to "level the playing field" for U.S. exporters.

Potential options for Congress include, but are not limited to, the following areas:

- **Structure of the Bank.** Congress could maintain the Ex-Im Bank as an independent agency, reorganize or privatize the functions of the Bank, or terminate the Bank.
- **Length of reauthorization.** Congress could extend the Bank's authority for a few years at a time (as in previous reauthorizations), for a longer period of time, or permanently reauthorize the Bank.
- **Bank's policies.** Congress could maintain the status quo, or revise the Bank's policies, such as those related to the requirements and limitations on the Ex-Im Bank's credit and insurance activities.
- **International ECA context.** Congress could seek to enhance international regulation of official export credit activity through the

OECD or other mechanisms, or enhance the Ex-Im Bank's understanding of international export credit activity and trends.

Most recently, Congress passed H.R. 2072 to extend the Bank's authority through FY2014; previously, the Bank's authority was extended to May 31, 2012. H.R. 2072 also raises the Bank's lending authority incrementally from the previous $100 billion limit to $140 billion in FY2014, contingent on certain other requirements. In addition, H.R. 2072, among other things, includes provisions related to the Bank's domestic content policy and requirements to conduct international negotiations to reduce and eliminate official export credit activity. Prior to final action, the 112th Congress considered several other bills related to the Ex-Im Bank's authority.

Chapter 3 – The U.S. Export-Import Bank (Ex-Im), the United States' official export credit agency (ECA), helps U.S. firms export goods and services by providing a range of financial products. Ex-Im, whose primary mission is to support jobs through exports, has a range of policy requirements, including support of small business. The Organisation for Economic Cooperation and Development (OECD) Arrangement governs aspects of U.S. and some foreign countries' ECAs. GAO examined (1) Ex-Im's mission and organization compared with ECAs from other Group of Seven (G-7) countries (major industrialized countries that consult on economic issues), (2) ExIm's policy requirements compared with other G-7 ECAs, (3) Ex-Im's domestic content policy compared with other G-7 ECAs, and (4) the OECD Arrangement's role in governing ECA activities.

In: The Export-Import Bank of the United States   ISBN: 978-1-62618-709-2
Editor: Fraser M. Mulder   © 2013 Nova Science Publishers, Inc.

Chapter 1

EXPORT-IMPORT BANK:
BACKGROUND AND LEGISLATIVE ISSUES[*]

Shayerah Ilias

SUMMARY

The Export-Import Bank of the United States (Ex-Im Bank, EXIM
Bank, or the Bank), an independent federal government agency, is the
official export credit agency (ECA) of the United States. It helps finance
U.S. exports of manufactured goods and services, with the objective of
contributing to the employment of U.S. workers, primarily in
circumstances when alternative financing is not available. The Ex-Im
Bank also may assist U.S. exporters to meet foreign, officially sponsored,
export credit competition. Its main programs are direct loans, loan
guarantees, working capital guarantees, and export credit insurance. Ex-
Im Bank transactions are backed by the full faith and credit of the U.S.
government. The Ex-Im Bank is a participant in President Obama's
National Export Initiative (NEI), a plan to double exports by 2015 to
support 2 million U.S. jobs. The Bank operates under a renewable
charter, the Export-Import Bank Act of 1945, as amended. The charter
requires that all of the Bank's financing have a reasonable assurance of
repayment and directs the Bank to supplement, and to not compete with,
private capital.

---

[*] This is an edited, reformatted and augmented version of Congressional Research Service,
Publication No. R42472, dated May 22, 2012.

In light of the international financial crisis, demand for Ex-Im Bank services has grown in recent years. In FY2011, the Bank approved more than 3,700 transactions of credit and insurance support, totaling about $33 billion—the highest level of authorizations in the history of the Bank. The Ex-Im Bank estimated that its credit and insurance activities supported about $41 billion in U.S. exports of goods and services, and were associated with 290,000 U.S. jobs, in FY2011.

The Ex-Im Bank has been "self-sustaining" for appropriations purposes since FY2008. It uses offsetting collections to cover its administrative expenses and program operations. Congress sets an upper limit on the level of the Bank's financial activities as part of the annual appropriations process. For FY2012, Congress appropriated $4 million for the Ex-Im Bank's Office of Inspector General (OIG), and authorized a limit of $58 million on the total amount that the Ex-Im Bank can spend on its credit and insurance programs and a limit of $89.9 million for the Bank's administrative expenses (P.L. 112-74). For FY2013, the President requested an appropriation of $4.4 million for the OIG, a limit of $38 million on the Bank's program activities, and a limit of $103.9 million for the Bank's administrative expenses. Since 1990, the Ex-Im Bank has retuned to the U.S. Treasury $4.9 billion more than it received in appropriations.

The Organization for Economic Cooperation and Development (OECD) "Arrangement on Export Credits" sets forth export credit terms and conditions, including restrictions on tied aid, for the activities of the Ex-Im Bank and the ECAs of foreign countries that are OECD members. Other OECD agreements set forth sector-specific rules, guidelines on environmental procedures, and other terms and conditions.

The 112th Congress has considered several pieces of legislation to renew the Ex-Im Bank's charter, which previously had been extended to May 31, 2012 (P.L. 112-74). Most recently, Congress has passed a bill to extend the Ex-Im Bank's authority through FY2014 (H.R. 2072). Members of Congress may examine issues related to the Ex-Im Bank that center on the economic rationale for the Bank; the impact of the Bank on the federal budget and U.S. taxpayers; the Bank's support for specific types of business or industries; the current balance between the Bank's advancement of U.S. commercial interests and other U.S. policy goals; the competitive position of the Bank compared to foreign ECAs; and the Bank's organizational structure.

INTRODUCTION

The Export-Import Bank of the United States (the Ex-Im Bank, the EXIM Bank, or the Bank) is an independent U.S. government executive agency and a wholly owned U.S. government corporation.[1] The Ex-Im Bank is the official export credit agency (ECA) of the United States, and is charged with financing and promoting exports of U.S. manufactured goods and services, with the objective of contributing to the employment of U.S. workers. It uses its authority and resources to provide export credit and insurance support to U.S. exporters primarily in circumstances when alternative financing is not available.

The Bank operates under a renewable charter, the Export-Import Bank Act of 1945, as amended.[2] Most recently, Congress has passed a bill to extend the Ex-Im Bank's authority through FY2014 (H.R. 2072). Previously, the Ex-Im Bank's charter had been extended to May 31, 2012 (P.L. 112- 74).

Ex-Im Bank's charter requires that all of the Bank's financing have a reasonable assurance of repayment and directs the Bank to supplement—and to not compete with—private capital. The Organization for Economic Cooperation and Development (OECD) Arrangement on Official Supported Export Credits (the "OECD Arrangement") guides the activities of the Ex-Im Bank and other foreign ECAs whose governments are members of the OECD.

In FY2011, the Bank approved more than 3,700 transactions of credit and insurance support, totaling about $33 billion—the highest level of authorizations in the history of the Bank. The ExIm Bank estimated that its credit and insurance activities supported about $41 billion in U.S. exports of goods and services, and were associated with 290,000 U.S. jobs, in FY2011.

Congress does not directly approve individual Ex-Im Bank transactions, but has a number of authorizing and oversight responsibilities concerning the Bank and its activities. Congress authorizes the Bank's legal charter for a period of time chosen by Congress. At times, Congress has required an annual reauthorization of the Bank's legal charter, and at other times has authorized the Bank for periods that have varied from two to five years. Congress also approves an annual appropriation for the Bank that sets an upper limit on the level of the Bank's financial activities. Congress can always amend or alter the Bank's governing legislation as it deems appropriate. Members of Congress and congressional committees can request that the Bank's President consult with them or testify before committees, with some qualifications. In addition, the Senate confirms presidential appointments to the Bank's Board of Directors.

This report discusses the Ex-Im Bank's domestic and international context, credit and insurance programs and activities, statutory and policy requirements for the Ex-Im Bank's transactions, and selected policy issues for Congress.

EX-IM BANK BUDGET

When the Ex-Im Bank was initially established, it was capitalized by an appropriation of $1 billion from the U.S. Treasury. The Bank also is authorized to borrow up to $6 billion directly from the Treasury, and it may draw upon a substantial line of credit with the Federal Financing Bank (FFB).[3] The Ex-Im Bank uses its Treasury borrowings to finance its short-term needs, and repays the Treasury quarterly from loan repayments and by borrowing from the FFB on a medium- and long-term basis. The Ex-Im Bank has been "self-sustaining" for appropriations purposes as of FY2008. Since then, in the President's annual budget request, the President has requested, and Congress has approved, that offsetting collections would count against the appropriation of subsidy and administrative expenses from the General Fund and that the net appropriation is expected to be $0. In essence, the President requests approval for the level of expenses that the Ex-Im Bank would cover on its own. At the start of the fiscal year, the U.S. Treasury provides the Ex-Im Bank with an "appropriation warrant" for program costs and administrative expenses. The amount of the warrant is established by the spending limits set by Congress in the appropriations process. The Ex-Im Bank retains the fees that it collects during the year that are in excess of expected losses ("offsetting collections"), and uses the offsetting collections to repay the warrant received at the start of the fiscal year, resulting in a net appropriation of $0. In essence, the Ex-Im Bank can receive funds from the U.S. Treasury and can repay those funds as offsetting collections come in. In recent years, the Ex-Im Bank has not received direct funds from the U.S. Treasury as part of the appropriations process. The Ex-Im Bank has been able to support its administrative and program expenses without an initial warrant from the Treasury at the start of the fiscal year, because of a combination of its early offsetting collections and carryover funds. Congress permits the Ex-Im Bank to maintain carryover funds, which are unused offsetting collections, for up to four years. In addition, the Ex-Im Bank has not borrowed from the FFB since FY1997.[4]

For FY2013, the President requested an appropriation of $4.4 million for the Ex-Im Bank's Office of Inspector General (OIG), a limit of $38 million on the total amount the Bank can spend on its credit and insurance programs, and a limit of $103.9 million for the Bank's administrative expenses (see Table 1). The President also requested that amounts collected by the Ex-Im Bank in excess of administrative and program obligations, up to $50 million, shall remain available until September 30, 2015, and that any excess above $50 million shall be deposited in the General Fund of the Treasury. For FY2012,

Congress appropriated $4 million for the Ex-Im Bank's OIG, and authorized a limit of $58 million on the total amount that the Ex-Im Bank can spend on its credit and insurance programs and a limit of $89.9 million for the Bank's administrative expenses. Congress also authorized that the Ex-Im Bank's offsetting collections in excess of obligations, of up to $50 million, shall remain available for use by the Ex-Im Bank until FY2015.[5]

Table 1. Budget of the Export-Import Bank, FY2008-2013
(in millions of dollars)

	FY08	FY09	FY10	FY11	FY12 Estimated	FY13 Requested
Inspector General Amount Requested	1	2.5	2.5	3	4	4.4
Inspector General Amount Appropriated	1	1	2.5	2.5	4	—
Total Subsidy Requested	68	41	58	93	76	38
Total Subsidy Appropriated	68	41	58	58	58	—
Total Administrative Budget Requested	78	82	84	106	125	104
Total Administrative Budget Appropriated	78	82	84	84	90	—
Operating Expenses	590	690	1,245	872	978	181
Direct Loan Subsidy	—	8	—	7	8	8
Loan Guarantee Subsidy	25	30	39	59	58	38
Reestimates of Subsidy Costs	487	570	1,122	718	793	—
Loan Modifications	2	—	—	—	—	—
Administrative Expenses	78	82	84	84	90	104
Budget Resources	934	1,031	1,923	1,829	1,814	1,391
Unobligated balance	346	342	324	679	953	836
Budget Authority (gross)	585	685	1,599	1,145	861	555
Appropriated	487	571	1,121	718	793	—
Other	123	158	478	427	68	555
Recoveries from previous years	3	4	—	5	—	—
Budget Authority (net)	462	527	1,121	443	393	—
Outlays (net)	468	511	748	153	506	-403

Source: Office of Management and Budget. *Budget of the United States Government*, various issues; Washington, U.S. Government Printing Office.

Note: Subsidy refers to program activities (the cost of direct loans, loan guarantees, insurance, and tied aid) conducted by the Ex-Im Bank. Reestimates of subsidy costs refer to reestimates of direct loan and loan guarantee subsidies and the interest on those reestimates.

The Ex-Im Bank had $701.1 million in offsetting collections in FY2011, up from $479.4 million in FY2010, that it used to cover its administrative and program expenses. Since 1990, the Ex-Im Bank has retuned to the U.S. Treasury $4.9 billion more than it received in appropriations.

Ex-Im Bank Budget History

The Omnibus Budget Reconciliation Act of 1990 (P.L. 101-508) included two sections with implications for the Ex-Im Bank's budget.

- Under the terms of the Budget Enforcement Act of 1990 (Title XIII), Congress appropriates the estimated amount of subsidy the Bank expects to expend throughout all of its credit programs, including direct loans, guarantees, and insurance. Congress no longer sets separate limits on the amount of loans, guarantees, and insurance the Bank can authorize, but the Bank continues to provide estimates of the amounts of activity it expects to undertake.
- Under the Federal Credit Reform Act of 1990 (Title V), for a given fiscal year, the cost of federal credit activities, including those of the Ex-Im Bank, is reported on an accrual basis equivalent with other federal spending, rather than on a cash flow basis, as used previously.[6] The Bank's estimates now allocate budgetary resources to reserve against the estimated risk of loss to the Bank.

EX-IM BANK ACTIVITY

Ex-Im Bank uses its authority and resources to (1) assume commercial and political risks that exporters or private financial institutions are unwilling, or unable, to undertake alone; (2) overcome maturity and other limitations in private sector export financing; and (3) assist U.S. exporters to meet foreign, officially sponsored, export credit competition.

Financial Products

Ex-Im Bank groups its financial products into four categories: (1) direct loans; (2) loan guarantees; (3) working capital guarantees; and (4) export credit insurance. It also has a number of special financing programs.

Ex-Im Bank charges interest, risk premia, and other fees for its services. Generally speaking, the Ex-Im Bank's credit exposure is limited to 80% of the value of the exported good, and the buyer must make a cash payment that is 15% of the total value of the export contract. The Ex-Im Bank determines repayment terms based on a number of variables, such as buyer, industry, and country conditions; terms of international rules on export credit activity; and the matching of terms offered by foreign ECAs. Repayment time frames are less than one year for short-term transactions, one to seven years for medium-term transactions, and greater than seven years for long-term transactions.[7]

Direct Loans

Under the Ex-Im Bank's direct loan program, the Ex-Im Bank offers loans directly to foreign buyers of U.S. goods and services. If the foreign borrower defaults, the Bank will pay the lender the outstanding principal and interest on the loan. The Ex-Im Bank extends to the U.S. company's foreign customer a loan covering up to 80% of the U.S. contract value. The direct loans carry fixed interest rates and generally are made at terms that are the most attractive allowed under the provisions of the OECD Arrangement on Export Credits, which sets minimum interest rate benchmarks. The Ex-Im Bank's direct loan transactions have no minimum or maximum size, but generally involve amounts of more than $10 million. The Bank also has an Intermediary Credit Program it uses to offer medium- and long-term fixed-rate financing to buyers of U.S. exports; U.S. exporters must face officially subsidized foreign competition to qualify for this program.

Prior to 1980, the Bank's direct lending program was its chief financing vehicle, which it used to finance such capital-intensive exports as commercial aircraft and nuclear power plants. Both the budget authority requested by the Administration and the level approved by Congress for the Bank's direct lending were sharply reduced during the 1980s. In the past decade, demand for ExIm Bank direct loans has been limited, because commercial interest rates were low. In light of the international financial crisis, the Ex-Im Bank has worked to increase access to direct loans by engaging with borrowers on a case-by-case basis to structure transactions to adapt to current financial conditions.

Tied Aid Capital Projects Fund

As part of its direct lending program, the Bank has a Tied Aid Capital Projects Fund (TACPF), often referred to as the tied aid "war chest," that it uses to counter specific projects that are receiving foreign officially subsidized export financing. The Ex-Im Bank may conduct tied aid transactions to counter attempts by foreign governments to sway purchases in favor of their exporters solely on the basis of subsidized financing, rather than on market conditions (price, quality, etc.). Tied aid credits and mixed credits are two methods whereby governments provide their exporters with official assistance to promote exports. Tied aid credits include loans and grants which reduce financing costs below market rates for exporters and which are tied to the procurement of goods and services from the donor country. Mixed credits combine concessional government financing (funds at below market rates or terms) with commercial or near-commercial funds to produce an overall rate that is lower than market-based interest rates and carries more lenient loan terms. The United States does tie substantial amounts of its agricultural and military aid to U.S. goods, but it generally has avoided using such financing to promote American capital goods exports. The amount of funds in the TACPF was $171 million in FY2010.

Funds for the tied aid war chest are available to the Bank from the Treasury Department and are subtracted from the Bank's direct credit resources. Applications for the tied aid fund are subject to review by the Treasury Department.

Loan Guarantees

Loan guarantees constitute the largest amount of Ex-Im Bank financing, by dollar value. The ExIm Bank uses loan guarantees to assist U.S. exporters by protecting against the commercial and political uncertainty of exporting. Loan guarantees by the Ex-Im Bank cover the repayment risk on the foreign buyer's debt obligations incurred in the purchase of U.S. exports. Through a loan guarantee, the Ex-Im Bank guarantees to a lender (U.S. or foreign) that makes a loan to a foreign buyer to purchase U.S. goods and services that, if the foreign borrower defaults, the Bank will pay the lender the outstanding principal and interest on the loan.

The Ex-Im Bank charges the foreign borrower a fee to guarantee the loan in a variable amount based on the duration, amount, and risk characteristics of the transaction. The Ex-Im Bank extends loan guarantees on a medium- and long-term basis.

The Ex-Im Bank's loan guarantee to a foreign buyer is typically used for financing purchases of U.S. capital equipment and services. The Ex-Im Bank's comprehensive guarantee covers commercial and political risks for up to 85% of the U.S. contract value.

Working Capital Guarantee Program

Ex-Im Bank's Working Capital Guarantee Program provides repayment guarantees to lenders (primarily commercial banks) on secured, short-term working capital loans made to qualified exporters. Working capital guarantees can be for a single loan or a revolving line of credit, and cover 90% of the outstanding balance of working capital loans to exporters supported by export-related inventory and accounts receivable. The Ex-Im Bank charges the borrower a fee to guarantee the loan based on duration, amount, and risk characteristics of the transaction. The program is intended to facilitate finance for businesses that have exporting potential but need working capital funds to produce or market their goods or services for export. Small businesses are the primary users of the Working Capital Guarantee Program.

In FY2010, the Ex-Im Bank launched a Supply-Chain Finance Guarantee Program, which is designed to support U.S. exporters and their U.S.-based suppliers, many of whom are small businesses. Under the program, lenders will purchase accounts receivable owned by suppliers and due from the exporter. The Ex-Im Bank provides 90% guarantee on repayment obligation. The program provides competitively priced working capital finance to U.S. suppliers of U.S. exporters. It may benefit "hidden exporters" such as U.S. small businesses that supply products or services to larger U.S. exporters.

Export Credit Insurance

Export credit insurance is another major product offered by the Ex-Im Bank. The Ex-Im Bank issues the insurance policy to a U.S. exporter, which provides credit to the foreign buyer of the exporter's products. If the foreign borrower defaults for political or commercial reasons, the Bank will pay the exporter the outstanding balance owed by the foreign borrower. Insurance coverage carries various conditions that must be met by the insured before the Bank will pay off a claim. The Ex-Im Bank charges the exporter an insurance premium in a variable amount based on duration, amount, and risk characteristics of transactions. The Ex-Im Bank's export credit insurance includes both short-term and medium-term insurance. Small businesses are a significant user of the Ex-Im Bank's export credit insurance program.

Like loan guarantees, export credit insurance reduces some of the risks involved in exporting by protecting against commercial or political uncertainty. There is an important distinction, however, between the two programs. Insurance coverage is more conditional than a guarantee. In contrast, a guarantee is a commitment made to a commercial bank by the Ex-Im Bank that promises full repayment with few, if any, conditions attached.

Special Financing Programs

The Ex-Im Bank's support for U.S. export sales also includes special financing programs that focus on a particular industry or financing technique, including:

- **Aircraft Finance.** The Ex-Im Bank offers financing for new or used U.S. manufactured commercial and general aviation aircraft under its direct loan, guarantee, and insurance programs. The Organization for Economic Cooperation and Development (OECD) Aircraft Sector Understanding ("OECD Aircraft Sector Understanding") generally sets the terms and conditions of the Ex-Im Bank's financing support for aircraft.
- **Project Finance.** The Ex-Im Bank offers limited recourse project finance to newly created companies. Project finance is an arrangement in which the creditworthiness of projects depends on their future cash flows, and these future cash flows are the source of repayment. Project finance typically covers large, long-term infrastructure and industrial projects.

Examples of Ex-Im Bank Transactions

Direct Loan. In August 2010, the Ex-Im Bank authorized a $159 million direct loan to Cerro de Hula Wind Farm, a utility-scale wind project in Honduras, for the purchase of 51 wind turbines from Gamesa Wind US LLC (Longhorne, PA). The Ex-Im Bank reported that the wind turbines would be manufactured using generators supplied by ABB Power T & D Company Inc. (Bland, VA), blades by LM Glassfiber Inc. (Grand Forks, ND), and equipment and services from other U.S. suppliers.

Loan Guarantee. In FY2011, the Ex-Im Bank authorized a long-term loan guarantee of close to $120 million to support a General Electric Transportation sale of locomotives to South Africa's Transnet Ltd., a South African train, port, and pipeline company headquartered in Johannesburg. Barclays Bank PLC, London is the guaranteed lender. Ten fully assembled GE Model C30ACi locomotives and U.S.-manufactured components for locomotive kits will be shipped from GE's Erie, PA, manufacturing facility to South Africa. In addition, the Bank approved a preliminary commitment for about $200 million for the purchase of more locomotives by Transnet.

Working Capital Guarantee. In September 2011, the Ex-Im Bank approved a $16.7 million working capital guarantee for the sale of exports by Quantum Reservoir Impact (QRI; Houston, TX) to Mexico, Kuwait, and other destination markets. QRI exports reservoir management equipment and services for the upstream sector of the oil and gas industry and also provides related engineering consulting services. Amegy Bank (Houston) is the lender of the working capital loan.

Export Credit Insurance. In April 2011, the Ex-Im Bank authorized $40 million in export credit insurance for BendTec., a small business (Duluth, MN), for the sale of fabricated high pressure piping, bends, and fittings to Technopromexport in Moscow, Russia. BendTec's products will be exported to India for installation at a super thermal power project.

Source: Ex-Im Bank, "Ex-Im Bank Provides $159 Million in Trade Finance for Pennsylvania Manufacturer To Export Turbines to Wind Farm in Honduras," press release, August 20, 2010, http://www.exim.gov /pressrelease.cfm/9F2BD5AC-FAFC-EE31-C412F9A785BF9C1E/; Ex-Im Bank, FY2011 Annual Report; Ex-Im Bank, "Ex-Im Bank Approves $100 Million In Financing For Sale Of GE Locomotives To South Africa's Transnet," press release, February 24, 2011, http://www.exim.gov /pressrelease.cfm/58EAE7B2-090D-E9CE4C77F09BA969CAA8/; and Ex-Im Bank, "Ex-Im Bank Approves Nearly $40 Million in Export Credit Insurance for Minnesota Small Business," press release, April 13, 2011, http://www.exim.gov/pressrelease.cfm/503C238F-F77DE980-A51E70B2028621E7/.

Activity Level

Authorizations

In FY2011, the Ex-Im Bank approved 3,751 transactions of credit and insurance support, which amounted to about $33 billion in authorizations—the third consecutive year of record high levels of authorizations for the Bank (see Table 2). The Ex-Im Bank estimated that credit and insurance activities supported about $41 billion in U.S. exports of goods and services in FY2011, up from $34 billion worth of exports estimated to have been supported in FY2010. The Ex-Im Bank also estimated that the exports supported by its financing were associated with 290,000 U.S. jobs in FY2011, up from 227,000 U.S. jobs in FY2010. The Ex-Im Bank finances less than 5% of U.S. exports annually. Notably, a significant portion of Ex-Im Bank financing is for exports of capital-intensive U.S. exports.

Table 2. The Ex-Im Bank's Credit and Insurance Authorizations,
FY2008-FY2011
(Millions of U.S. Dollars)

	Number of Authorizations			Amount Authorized		
Program	2009	2010	2011	2009	2010	2011
Total Financing						
Loans	16	15	18	$3,033	$4,261	$6,323
Loan Guarantees	619	719	784	$11,475	$13,106	$19,400
Medium- and Long-Term	146	162	178	$9,943	$10,927	$16,172
Working Capital	473	557	606	$1,531	$2,179	$3,228
Insurance	2,256	2,798	2,949	$11,474	$7,101	$7,004
Total Authorizations	**2,891**	**3,532**	**3,751**	**$21,021**	**$24,468**	**$32,727**
Selected Types of Financing						
Exports by Small Business	2,540	3,091	3,247	$4,360	$5,053	$6,037
Percent of Total	87.9%	87.5%	86.6%	20.7%	20.7%	18.4%
Environmentally Beneficial						
Exports	88	108	142	$394	$536	$890
Percent of Total	3.0%	3.1%	3.8%	1.9%	2.2%	2.7%
Renewable Energy Exports	13	27	45	$93	$332	$721
Percent of Total	0.4%	0.8%	1.2%	0.4%	1.4%	2.2%
Exports to Sub-Saharan Africa	109	129	170	$412	$813	$1,381
Percent of Total	3.8%	3.7%	4.5%	2.0%	3.3%	4.2%

Source: Ex-Im Bank Annual Reports data adapted by CRS.
Note: The Ex-Im Bank distinguishes between financing for "environmentally beneficial" and "renewable energy" exports.

A number of factors have driven the surge in Ex-Im Bank activity in recent years. One major driver has been the international financial crisis and global economic downturn that began in 2007 and led to a decline in private sector export finance. As a result, the Ex-Im Bank witnessed a greater demand from U.S. exporters for its assistance to fill in the gaps in private sector financing. The Ex-Im Bank has noted that small businesses especially have faced difficulty accessing credit during the crisis. In response to the commercial and liquidity shortages associated with the global financial crisis, the Ex-Im Bank has taken several actions to enhance its financing products. In October 2008, the Bank started offering U.S. small businesses a 15% premium-rate reduction for certain insurance policies. The Bank also took measures to expand coverage under and to provide flexible financing terms for its Working Capital Guarantee Program. In addition, the Bank has worked to increase access to direct loans by engaging with borrowers on a case-by-case basis to structure transactions to adapt to the current financial conditions.

Another element driving demand for Ex-Im Bank services has been the changing international landscape of export financing. The growing number of players and volumes of export credit activity in the international export finance market has resulted in greater and varied competition for U.S. exporters, both from developed countries and from rising economic powers as they move up the value chain.[12] U.S. companies are seeking Ex-Im Bank assistance to help level the playing field and counter the officially backed export credit financing that their competitors receive from their ECAs.

Exposure

Congress sets limitations in the Ex-Im Bank's charter on the aggregate amounts of loan, guarantees, and insurance that the Ex-Im Bank can have outstanding at any one time (oftentimes referred to as the Ex-Im Bank's exposure cap/ceiling/limit).[8] The outstanding principal amount of all loans made, guaranteed, or insured by the Ex-Im Bank is charged at the full value against the limitation.

The Ex-Im Bank initially was capitalized with a stock of $1 billion in 1934. When Congress established the Ex-Im Bank as an independent agency in 1945, it authorized a limit on the Ex-Im Bank's outstanding aggregate credit and insurance authority that was no greater than three and one-half times the Bank's authorized stock of $1 billion. In 1951, Congress changed the statutory formula to four and one-half times the authorized stock. In 1954, Congress changed the outstanding limit from a formula calculation to $5 billion, and since then, has periodically enacted legislation that has increased the Bank's outstanding limitation (see Table 3).

H.R. 2072, the most recent Ex-Im Bank reauthorization bill passed by Congress, increases Ex-Im Bank's exposure cap incrementally from the previous limitation of $100 billion. H.R. 2072 increases Ex-Im Bank's exposure cap to $120 billion in FY2012, $130 billion in FY2013, and $140 billion in FY2014, with the increase in the exposure cap for FY2013 and FY2014 contingent on the Bank maintaining a default rate of less than 2% and on meeting various reporting requirements.

In FY2011, the Bank's total exposure stood at about $89 billion, up from $75 billion in FY2010. As the Bank's activities have grown, the Bank's exposure level also has grown. In FY2011, the Ex-Im Bank had exposure for its credit and insurance activities in 171 countries, across different geographical areas and industrial sectors.

The composition of the Ex-Im Bank's exposure portfolio by geographical area has remained relatively stable in recent years.

Table 3. Legislative Changes to the Export-Import Bank's Limit on Outstanding Aggregate Credit and Insurance Authority

Year	Legislation	New Limit Resulting from Legislation
1945	P.L. 79-173	Three and one-half times the authorized stock of $1 billion
1951	P.L. 82-158	Four and one-half times the authorized stock of $1 billion
1954	P.L. 83-570	$5 billion
1958	P.L. 85-424	$7 billion
1963	P.L. 88-101	$9 billion
1968	P.L. 90-267	$13.5 billion
1971	P.L. 92-126	$20 billion
1975	P.L. 93-646	$25 billion
1978	P.L. 95-630	$40 billion
1992	P.L. 102-429	$75 billion
2002	P.L. 107-189	Incremental increases in limit to $100 billion[a]
2012	H.R. 2072	Incremental increase in limit to $140 billion, contingent on certain requirements[b]

Source: U.S. Code notes; Lexis Nexis; and Jordan Jay Hillman, *The Export-Import Bank at Work* (Westport 1982).

[a] The Export-Import Bank Reauthorization Act of 2002 (P.L. 107-189) increased the Bank's exposure cap to $80 billion in FY2002, $85 billion in FY2003, $90 billion in FY2004, $95 billion in FY2005, and $100 billion in FY2006.

[b] The Export-Import Bank Reauthorization Act of 2012 (H.R. 2072) increases the Bank's exposure cap to $120 billion in FY2012, $130 billion in FY2013, and $140 billion in FY2014—with the increase in lending authority in FY2013 and FY2014 contingent on the Bank maintaining a "default rate" of less than 2% and on submitting various reports.

Asia has accounted for the largest portion of exposure, with significant Ex-Im Bank exposure in China and India. Latin America and the Caribbean have accounted for the second-largest portion of exposure, with major country markets being Brazil, Colombia, and Mexico. As for the composition of the Ex-Im Bank's portfolio by industrial sector, the air transportation sector historically has accounted for the largest portion of the Ex-Im Bank's exposure. Oil and gas generally has followed. However, in FY2010, manufacturing surpassed oil and gas as the second-largest source of Ex-Im Bank exposure and maintained second place in FY2011. Figures 1 and 2 show the Bank's total exposure in FY2011 by geographical area and industrial sector.

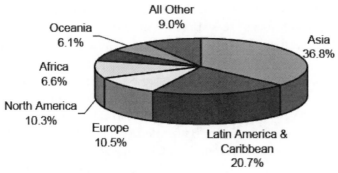

Source: Ex-Im Bank, *2011 Annual Report*.
Note: Total exposure for the Ex-Im Bank was $89 billion in FY2011.

Figure 1. Exposure by Geographical Area, FY2011.

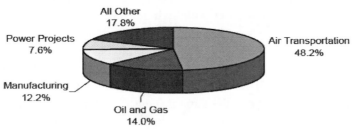

Source: Ex-Im Bank, *2011 Annual Report*.
Note: Total exposure for the Ex-Im Bank was $89 billion in FY2011.

Figure 2. Exposure by Industrial Sector, FY2011.

Credit Risks and Loan Repayment

Ex-Im Bank's default rate net of recoveries has been less than 2% of its loan disbursements and shipments guaranteed. The Bank closely monitors credit and other risks to its portfolio. The overall weighted-average risk rating for new authorizations improved in FY2011 for short-, medium-, and long-term export credit authorizations. The improvement in the risk rating primarily was due to the decrease in Ex-Im Bank-supported financing among borrowers that were rated higher-risk.[9]

Focus Areas

The Ex-Im Bank has identified country-specific and sector-specific areas in which to focus its credit and insurance activities. While the Ex-Im Bank operates in 175 countries around the world, it has identified nine emerging markets as primary focus areas: Brazil, Colombia, India, Indonesia, Mexico, Nigeria, South Africa, Turkey, and Vietnam. The Ex-Im Bank has chosen these markets based on several factors, including the size of their export markets for U.S. companies, their projected economic growth, their expected infrastructure needs, and the Ex-Im Bank's current level of activity in these markets.[10] In FY2011, these nine priority markets represented about 38% (about $12 billion) of the Ex-Im Bank's total authorizations and 33% (about $29 billion) of the Ex-Im Bank's total exposure. The Ex-Im Bank has identified infrastructure projects in foreign countries as a significant opportunity for U.S. exports of goods and services. In FY2011, the Ex-Im Bank provided more than $23 billion in infrastructure-related financing.[11]

The transactions included projects in sectors such as transportation, power generation, and mining. In terms of specific industries, the Ex-Im Bank has identified several industries with high potential for U.S. export growth in the nine priority markets. These industries are agribusiness, aircraft and avionics, construction, medical technologies, mining, oil and gas, and power generation (including renewable energy). In FY2011, these key industries represented close to 70% (about $23 billion) of the Ex-Im Bank's total authorizations. In that year, the aircraft industry, a historically major area of Ex-Im Bank financing, represented nearly 40% (about $13 billion) of the Ex-Im Bank's total authorizations.[12]

Statutory and Policy Requirements

A number of factors affect the Ex-Im Bank's participation in a particular credit or insurance transaction. Many of these factors or conditions are determined by Congress. The statutory and policy criteria that Ex-Im Bank financing support must meet include:

- **Reasonable Assurance of Repayment.** The Ex-Im Bank charter requires that all of the Bank's financing have a reasonable assurance of repayment.
- **Private Capital.** The charter directs the Ex-Im Bank to supplement, and to not compete with, private capital.
- **Economic Impact.** Congress requires that Ex-Im Bank projects have no adverse effect on U.S. industry. Chiefly, the Ex-Im Bank may not support projects that enable foreign production of an exportable good

that would compete with U.S. production of a same, or similar, good and that would cause "substantial injury" to U.S. producers. The Ex-Im Bank also may not support projects that result in the foreign production of a good that is substantially the same as a good subject to specified U.S. trade measures, such as anti-dumping or countervailing duty investigations.

- **Environmental Impact.** The Bank considers the potential beneficial or adverse effects of proposed transactions. The Ex-Im Bank's charter authorizes the Bank to grant or withhold financing support after taking into account the environmental impact of the proposed transaction.

- **Content.** Content is the amount of domestic and foreign costs from labor, materials, overhead, and other inputs associated with the production of an export. The Ex-Im Bank places certain limits on the maximum amount of foreign content that can be included in the transactions it supports. The Ex-Im Bank's content policy limits its support, for all medium- and long-term transactions, to the lesser of (1) 85% of the value of all goods and services contained within a U.S. supply contract or (2) 100% of the U.S. content of an export contract. In effect, in order to receive full Ex-Im Bank financing for an export transaction, the minimum domestic content requirement is 85% and the maximum foreign content allowance is 15%. If the foreign content exceeds 15%, then the Bank's support would be reduced.

- **Local Costs.** Local costs are the project-related costs for goods and services that are incurred in the buyer's country. When the Ex-Im Bank provides medium- or long-term financing for U.S. exports for foreign projects, it may also provide local cost support. Specifically, the Ex-Im Bank can support up to 30% of the value of the U.S. exports for goods and services that are originated and/or manufactured in the buyer's country, subject to certain requirements.

- **Military.** The Ex-Im Bank is prohibited by law from financing military items.

- **Shipping.** Certain products supported by the Ex-Im Bank must be transported exclusively on U.S. vessels. Under limited conditions, a waiver on this condition may be granted.

- **Nonfinancial or Noncommercial Considerations.** The Bank is allowed to deny applications for credit on the basis of nonfinancial and noncommercial considerations in cases where the President, in consultation with the House Financial Services Committee and Senate

Banking, Housing and Urban Affairs Committee, determines that the denial of such applications would advance U.S. national interests in areas such as international terrorism, nuclear proliferation, environmental protection, and human rights.[13]

The power to make such a determination has been delegated to the Secretary of State.[14]

- **Co-Financing.** The Ex-Im Bank enables financing with ECAs in other countries through "one-stop-shop" co-financing facilities (arrangements that allow products and services from two or more countries to benefit from a single ECA financing package).
- **Country Restrictions.** The charter prohibits the Bank from extending credit and insurance to certain countries, including those that are in armed conflict with the United States or with balance of payment problems.
- **Small Business.** The charter requires the Bank to make available not less than 20% of its aggregate loan, guarantee, and insurance authority to finance exports directly by U.S. small businesses.[15]
- **Renewable Energy.** The charter requires the Bank to promote the export of U.S. goods and services related to renewable energy sources.[16] In recent years, appropriations language further has specified the Bank should make available not less than 10% of its aggregate credit and insurance authority for the financing of exports of renewable energy technologies or energy efficient end-use technologies.
- **Sub-Saharan Africa.** The Ex-Im Bank's charter directs the Bank to promote the expansion of the Bank's financial commitments in sub-Saharan Africa, but does not include any quantitative target.

Ex-Im Bank Role in Federal Government Efforts to Promote Exports

Ex-Im Bank is one of approximately 20 federal agencies involved in U.S. government export promotion efforts.[17] Although the Ex-Im Bank is considered the official ECA of the United States, there are other federal agencies, such as the U.S. Department of Agriculture (USDA) and the Small Business Administration (SBA), that also conduct some export financing as part of their activities. The Ex-Im Bank is distinguished because it is the lead agency for providing financing and insurance for exports of U.S. manufactured goods and services, although it also provides financing for some agricultural exports. In addition, the Ex-Im Bank provides export financing for all types of businesses, both large and small. In contrast, USDA takes the lead on agricultural export financing, and SBA provides some export financing to small businesses. Ex-Im Bank plays a key role in the National Export Initiative (NEI), a plan launched by President Obama to double U.S. exports in five years to support 2 million jobs in the United States. Since 2010, overall U.S. exports of goods and service have increased at an annualized rate of 15.6%, a rate greater than the 15% required to double exports in five years.[18] Ex-Im Bank is involved in interagency bodies to coordinate federal export promotion activities. It is a part of the U.S. Trade Promotion Coordinating Committee (TPCC), an interagency committee created by the Export Enhancement Act of 1992 (P.L. 102-429). The TPCC, chaired by the Department of Commerce, is tasked with coordinating the export promotion and financing activities of federal agencies, including the Ex-Im Bank, and proposing an annual unified budget on federal trade promotion.[19] The Ex-Im Bank also is a member of the Export Promotion Cabinet (EPC), a Cabinet-level body that was established by the NEI and is composed of heads of federal agencies with export promotion functions and senior White House advisors. The EPC is charged with developing and coordinating the implementation of the NEI, in conjunction with the TPCC.

THE EX-IM BANK IN AN INTERNATIONAL CONTEXT

International Export Credit Activity

As international trade has grown, exporting financing has expanded. It is now a trillion-dollar market that supports approximately 10% of global trade.[20] It consists of private lenders and insurers, who operate commercially, and official ECAs.

Private lenders and insurers conduct the majority of short-term export financing, whereas ECAs are more heavily involved in medium- and long-term (MLT) export financing, including financing involving complex, multi-billion dollar sales such as aircraft and infrastructure projects. Most developed countries and many developing countries have ECAs. The role of ECAs has become more prominent in recent years due to the international financial crisis and global economic downturn in 2008 and the growing trade by emerging economies.

Table 4. Officially Supported New Medium- and Long-Term Export Credit Volumes by G-7 Countries and Selected Emerging Economies (Billions of U.S. dollars)

Country	ECA	2006	2007	2008	2009	2010
G-7 Countries						
Canada	Export Development Canada (EDC)	0.2	0.5	1.5	2.0	2.5
France	Compagnie Française d'Assurance pour le Commerce Extérieur	7.3	10.1	8.6	17.8	17.4
	(COFACE)					
Germany	Euler Hermes	13.3	8.9	10.8	12.9	22.5
Italy	S.p.A. Servizi Assicurativi del	4.0	3.5	7.6	8.2	5.3
	Commercio Estero (SACE)					
Japan	Japan Bank for International	2.4	1.8	1.5	2.7	2.9
	Cooperation (JBIC), Nippon Export and Investment Insurance (NEXI)					
United Kingdom	Export Credits Guarantee	0.6	0.4	0.8	1.4	1.9
	Department (ECGD)					
United States	Export-Import Bank of the United	8.6	8.2	11.0	17.0	13.0
	States (Ex-Im Bank)					
Total G-7		*36.3*	*33.4*	*41.8*	*62.0*	*65.4*
Emerging Economies						
Brazil	Brazilian Development Bank (BNDES), Seguradora Brasileira Crédito à	7.5	7.0	7.6	10.5	18.2
	Exportação (SBCE)					
China	Export-Import Bank of China, Sinosure, China Development Bank	22.0	33.0	52.0	51.1	45.0
	(CDB)					
India	Export-Import Bank of India, Export	5.6	8.5	8.7	7.3	9.5
	Credit Guarantee Corporation of India (ECGC)					
Total Brazil, China, India		*35.1*	*48.5*	*68.3*	*68.9*	*72.7*

Source: Data on export credit volumes from the Ex-Im Bank, Report to the U.S. Congress on Export Credit Competition and the Export-Import Bank of the United States, For the Period January 1, 2010 through December 31, 2010, Washington, DC, June 2011.

Notes: The Ex-Im Bank Competitiveness Report states that, for the G-7 countries, the Bank attempted to differentiate the standard, officially supported export credits that are regulated by the OECD Arrangement and export credits that are not subject to the OECD Arrangement. The competitiveness report also states that data on export credit volumes for Brazil, China, and India are approximations of activity based on available information and may be overstated due to the analytic assumptions used by the Bank.

Between 2006 and 2010, new MLT official export credit financing conducted by the G-7 countries as a whole nearly doubled, growing from $36.3 billion in 2006 to $65.4 billion in 2010. The United States represented 20% ($13 billion) of total new MLT financing by the G-7 countries in 2010, behind Germany and France. In comparison, during the same 2006-2010 period, new MLT official export credit financing conducted by Brazil, China, and India combined more than doubled, growing from $37 billion in 2006 to $72.7 billion in 2010. China alone accounted for $45 billion of new MLT official export credit financing in 2010 (see Table 4).[21]

Compared to the other ECAs, the sheer magnitude of China's official export credit financing is exceptional. For instance, China has supported Huawei, a Chinese telecommunications manufacturer, with a $30 billion credit line from the Chinese Development Bank (CDB).[22] China's support for this one company is comparable to total Ex-Im Bank financing in FY2011 (about $33 billion).

International Rules on Official Export Credit Activity

The Organization for Economic Cooperation and Development (OECD) Arrangement on Official Supported Export Credits (the "OECD Arrangement") guides the activities of the Ex-Im Bank and other foreign ECAs whose governments are members of the OECD (generally developed countries). The United States generally opposes subsidies for exports of commercial products. Since the 1970s, the United States has led efforts within the OECD to adopt international protocols which reduce the subsidy level in export credits by raising the interest rates on government-provided export credits to more closely reflect market levels.

The OECD Arrangement, which came into effect in April 1978, has been revised a number of times over the years. For example, participants have agreed over time to tighten restrictions on the use of tied aid. The participants agreed that projects would be financially viable, and commercial credits would be prohibited from using tied or partially untied aid credits, except for credits to the least developed countries where per capita income is below $2,465. Moreover, the agreement set up tests and consultation procedures to distinguish between projects that should be financed on market or official export credit terms, and those that legitimately require such aid funds. In addition, sector understandings govern the terms and conditions of exports in certain sectors, such as civilian aircraft.

OECD member countries also have agreed to other guidelines for official export credit. For example, in 2007, members agreed to revise guidelines on environmental procedures, referred to as "Common Approaches on Environment and Officially Supported Export Credits" (the "Common Approaches"). These environmental guidelines call for member governments to review projects for potential environmental impacts; to assess them against international standards, such as those of the World Bank; and to provide more public disclosure for environmentally sensitive projects. The OECD also adopted new guidelines on sustainable lending principles that aim to help developing countries avoid a renewed build-up of debt after receiving debt relief.

In addition, under the OECD, the United States and several European countries have agreed to an informal "home market rule" specific to the aircraft sector. Under this rule, the Ex-Im Bank and the ECAs of the United Kingdom, France, Spain, and Germany (which provide financing to Airbus) have agreed to limit access to officially supported export financing for the purchase of aircraft in their own domestic market and in each other's "home markets."[23]

Export credit financing that is covered by the OECD Arrangement generally is exempt from the World Trade Organization (WTO) Agreement on Subsidies and Countervailing Measures (SCM), which disciplines the use of subsidies, and it regulates the actions countries can take to counter the effects of these subsidies. The SCM Agreement language is interpreted to indicate that, for non-agricultural products, an export credit practice in conformity with the OECD Arrangement on export credits shall not be considered as an export subsidy prohibited by the SCM Agreement.

Unregulated Official ECA Activity

The OECD Arrangement does not cover all of the officially supported export credit activity conducted by all countries. Rising economic powers, such as China, Brazil, and India, are not members of the OECD (though they may have observer status during some OECD meetings and the OECD has offered them "enhanced engagement" with a view toward possible accession) and are not party to the OECD Arrangement. As such, the officially supported export credit activities of these countries may not comply with international export credit standards. [11] For example, China, Brazil, and India may offer below-market and concessionary financing alternatives with which it is difficult for ECAs of OECD members to compete. According to the Ex-Im Bank, non-OECD countries are expected to continue "expanding their market share by using exceptional financing methods, that comport with WTO provisions, but that are outside of the purview of the OECD rules, further expanding the scope of unregulated financing vis-à-vis constant volumes of OECD Arrangement-compliant activity." Officially subsidized export credit activity by emerging economies may increase in strategic markets, such as oil and gas, renewable energy, and natural resources extraction. For instance, Chinese ECAs "have shown strong signs of growing usage of export credits for export promotion purposes, especially in Africa, where they were offering preferential loans either in exchange for much needed resources (e.g., oil) or low cost loans on very extended repayment terms on projects in order to gain market share."[24] In addition, the ECAs of countries that are members of the OECD also conduct export credit financing and other activities that fall outside of the OECD Arrangement. There has been growth in unregulated forms of financing, that is, those that are not governed by the OECD Arrangement or any other international guidelines. One form of unregulated financing is the "market window," which is a government-owned entity or program that offers export credits on market terms. Market windows generally do not operate on purely commercial terms, as they tend to receive benefits from their government status that commercial lenders cannot access. Many ECAs operate market windows, such as Canada, Germany, and Italy; the United States does not have one. It is difficult to obtain data on market window operations of foreign countries. Another form of unregulated financing is untied lending support, which is credit support extended by a government entity to a recipient for the purpose of providing credit for strategic interests of the donor country. Because the untied loan is not tied to exports, it is not subject to the OECD export credit guidelines. Unregulated officially backed export credit financing is on the rise among both OECD and non-OECD countries. The increasing volumes of their official export credit activity that fall outside of the OECD Arrangement have raised concerns among OECD members about the effectiveness of the OECD Arrangement. The United States is engaging in efforts to negotiate export credit guidelines with China. During Chinese Vice President Xi Jinping's visit to the United States in February 2012, the United States and China announced that they would establish an international working group composed of export financing providers with the goal of completing a new set of export credit guidelines by 2014. These new guidelines would be aimed at replacing the current OECD Arrangement. It is unclear if membership in the working group would include major providers of official export financing that are not a part of the OECD, such as Brazil and India.[25]

U.S. Response to "Noncompetitive" Financing

On February 17, 2012, President Obama instructed the Ex-Im Bank "to give American companies a fair shot by matching the unfair export financing that their competitors receive from other countries," such as China.[26] In doing so, the President will employ existing authorities so that the Ex-Im Bank can provide U.S. firms compete for domestic or third-country sales with matching financing support to counter foreign "noncompetitive" financing that fails to observe international export credit disciplines under the OECD.[27]

The authority for matching such financing comes from the Ex-Im Bank's charter. One provision in the charter states that, if foreign countries offer financing for export sales in the United States under terms that do not comply with the OECD Arrangement ("noncompetitive financing"), the Secretary of the Treasury may authorize the Ex-Im Bank to provide financing for sales in the United States that matches the terms available through the foreign ECA (12 U.S.C. 635a-3). A second provision in the Ex-Im Bank's Charter authorizes the Ex-Im Bank to provide financing at rates which are competitive with those provided by foreign ECAs (12 U.S.C.a-1(b)). While this second provision does not explicitly mention the matching option, it could be viewed as giving the Bank flexibility in determining if foreign ECA financing is placing U.S. businesses at a competitive disadvantage, even when complying with the OECD Arrangement.[28] Ex-Im Bank could reportedly use this authority to match financing that Canada's ECA may offer to U.S. airlines for the purchase of the Bombardier's C-series aircraft, which could compete with Boeing's 737. Canada does not abide by the home market rule. Prior to the President's announcement, the Ex-Im Bank has used this policy once, to match financing with China for locomotive exports to Pakistan. In 2010, the Ex-Im Bank agreed to a $477 million financing deal to match China's financing terms in order to entice the Pakistani government to buy 150 General Electric Company locomotives. China offered financing terms for the export of Chinese railcars to Pakistan that were cheaper than those allowed by the OECD Arrangement on Export Credits. The matching deal required the Ex-Im Bank to work with the OECD. The deal has not been finalized.[29] It is not clear what impact, if any, possible repeated actions by the United States to match financing that is not compliant with the OECD may have on the rules-based system of the OECD Arrangement, or on the Ex-Im Bank's loan portfolio.[30]

SELECTED ISSUES FOR CONGRESS

Economic Debate

One rationale for the Ex-Im Bank is the acknowledged competition among nations' official export credit agencies. Some Ex-Im Bank supporters maintain that the Bank's programs are necessary for U.S. exporters to compete with foreign export financing and also to pressure foreign governments to eliminate concessionary financing. Another rationale cited by proponents of the Ex-Im Bank is the Bank's role in addressing market failures, such as imperfect information and barriers to entry. Supporters stress that deficiencies in financial markets bias those markets against exports of high-value, long-term assets. Others, including some economists, view government-funded export financing efforts as a subsidy which distorts free markets, because they encourage commercial activities that are not commercially viable, and in doing so, may encourage an inefficient use of resources. While critics concede that federal export assistance may help individual firms, they contend that such activities do not influence the overall level of employment and may, in fact, simply shift production among sectors within the economy in the long run. Critics also assert that macroeconomic factors, such as global economic growth and exchange rates, hold greater sway over a nation's level of exports. Some opponents also argue that, by providing financing or insurance for exporters that the market seems unwilling, or unable, to provide, Ex-Im Bank activities draw from the financial resources within the economy that would be available for other uses.

U.S. Airlines' Lawsuit Against the Ex-Im Bank

In recent months, debate about the economic impact of Ex-Im Bank activities has been driven in part by a charge by Delta Airlines and other U.S. airlines, led by the Air Transport Association of America (ATAA), that Ex-Im Bank financing for Boeing aircraft exports to India and other countries has led to an oversupply of airline seats that has had an adverse effect on their businesses.

The group also has charged that the Ex-Im Bank's economic impact analysis procedures are inconsistent with the Bank's charter. Delta and these other airlines have filed a legal challenge against the Ex-Im Bank seeking an injunction on Ex-Im Bank loan guarantees to Air India. Following a federal judge's denial for a preliminary injunction that would stop Ex-Im Bank financing of Boeing exports to India, the airlines filed a motion on February 1, 2012, for a judgment on the merits of the case, which is being heard by the U.S. District Court for the District of Columbia.

U.S. companies that purchase planes and other products are not able to access assistance from the Ex-Im Bank, but may obtain financing from the ECAs of other countries. For example, Delta purchases planes from Boeing, but may not use Ex-Im Bank financing for those purchases. However, Delta has used officially backed export financing for its purchases of airplanes from Canada's Bombardier Inc. or Brazil's Embraer S.A.

Sources: "Airlines Press Ahead With Ex-Im Bank Lawsuit After Judge Denies Injunction," *Inside U.S. Trade's World Trade Online*, February 9, 2012. Josh Mitchell and Corey Boles, "Boeing, Delta Clash on Exports," *The Wall Street Journal*, March 16, 2012.

"Corporate Welfare" Debate

A long-standing concern about the Ex-Im Bank centers on "corporate welfare" issues, with some observers critical that the bulk of Ex-Im Bank financing, by dollar value, historically has been directed to a few large U.S. corporations that they believe are capable of shouldering the risks of exporting to developing countries. Some critics of the Ex-Im Bank have called it "Boeing's Bank," in reference to the fact that Boeing Corporation, a U.S. aerospace company, historically has been the single largest beneficiary of Ex-Im Bank support. In FY2011, about 56% of Ex-Im Bank loans and long-term guarantees, by dollar value, supported the sale of Boeing aircraft to foreign countries, down from about 63% in FY2010 and 88% in FY2009.[31]

Supporters point out that the Ex-Im Bank's mission is to support U.S. businesses of all sizes and that the Bank places special emphasis on supporting small business. They note that, although small businesses have accounted for about 20% of Ex-Im Bank support by dollar *value*, they have accounted for more than 80% of the total *number* of transactions conducted by the Ex-Im Bank in recent years.[32] Some supporters may argue that focusing on the dollar value of Ex-Im Bank support to small businesses may be misleading, because the larger size of corporations naturally results in a scale of business that requires larger volumes of support. In addition, some supporters may point out that Ex-Im Bank data may not reflect all of the small businesses who benefit from Ex-Im Bank services, such as "invisible" exporters who provide goods and services used by other companies that directly export. For example, many of the inputs that Boeing uses for its aircraft are sourced from small businesses across the United States. Some critics do not make a distinction between large and small business support, remaining opposed to the notion of taxpayer funds being directed toward private benefits. Some critics of government export promotion programs suggest that the private sector may be more well-suited and efficient than the federal government for leading such activities. In response, some contend that the federal government plays a unique role in its capacity to address market failures, such as imperfect information, which dampen the level of U.S. exports. They also contend that federal financing of exports is critical in times of financial crisis, which can lead to a shortfall in the private sector financing.

Impact on U.S. Taxpayers

While the Ex-Im Bank is a self-sustaining agency that receives a net appropriation of zero from Congress, a point of contention is the risk to taxpayers imposed by the Bank's activities. Opponents argue that because Ex-Im Bank loans are backed by the full faith and credit of the U.S. government, taxpayers are potentially burdened if the Bank's projects fail. Supporters point out that a reasonable assurance of repayment is required by the Bank's charter for all credit authorizations and that the Bank monitors credit and other risks in its portfolio. In addition, supporters may point out that, since 1990, the Ex-Im Bank has retuned to the U.S. Treasury $4.9 billion more than it received in appropriations.

Congressional Directives to Support Specific Sectors

Another set of ongoing issues regarding the Ex-Im Bank centers on congressional directives that require the Ex-Im Bank to support exports in specific sectors, namely exports of small businesses and exports of "green technologies." These also are areas that have been identified as sectors of focus under the NEI. One issue is the extent to which the Ex-Im Bank has been able to fulfill these mandates. For example, the Senate committee report for FY2011 State-Foreign Operations appropriations (S.Rept. 111-237) expresses concern that, according to the Government Accountability Office, the Ex-Im Bank "has fallen far short of the congressional directive to allocate 10 percent of its annual financing to renewable energy or energy efficiency technologies, and that financing for fossil fuel projects continues to far exceed that for clean energy." However, supporters point out that the Ex-Im Bank is largely a demand-driven agency. While the Ex-Im Bank can make financing available for certain purposes, such as small business or "green" technology financing (as it already has), if U.S. firms do not have sufficient interests or commercial incentives for exporting in particular markets, then they may not seek out Ex-Im Bank support. More fundamental is a question about whether or not Congress should direct the Ex-Im Bank to target its support to specific sectors. Some observers support targeting federal export assistance to certain U.S. exporters and industries and for certain geographic markets that have high export potential and value. These exporting sectors and markets also may be the ones in which federal support makes the most difference. For example, environmentally friendly and energy-efficient goods and services often rely on newer forms of technology and entail perhaps greater risks than other types of exports, which may result in reluctance in the private sector to support such exports. Consequently, federal financing and support for "green" exports may boost their levels. However, some critics of targeted forms of export assistance contend that such policies essentially are a mechanism whereby the federal government determines "winners and losers" in the market. They contend that such action can lead to economic distortions and harm other productive U.S. firms. Some also may be concerned that such mandates may constrain the activities of the Bank.

International Competitiveness of the Ex-Im Bank

Concerns about the international competitiveness of the Ex-Im Bank generally have been twofold. One set of issues centers on the impact of the Ex-Im Bank's statutory and policy requirements on the competitive position of Ex-Im Bank financing for U.S businesses. The Ex-Im Bank may face a challenge of advancing U.S. commercial interests overseas while supporting other U.S. public policy goals.[33] According to the Ex-Im Bank's 2011 competitiveness report, the Ex-Im Bank generally maintained its competitiveness relative to the ECAs of the G-7 countries in terms of its core business policies and practices (such as Ex-Im Bank coverage, interest rates, exposure fee rates, and risk premia). However, the report stated that U.S. exporters and lenders have expressed concern that certain Ex-Im Bank policy requirements, upon which the Ex-Im Bank conditions whether or not to support a transaction, may have an adverse effect on the Ex-Im Bank's international competitiveness. For example:

- **Economic impact analysis.** While all G-7 ECAs have a broad mandate to support transactions that benefit their domestic economy, and base their decision to provide support on economic impact, the Ex-Im Bank is the only ECA that is required by law to use an economic impact analysis to weigh the costs and benefits of support to an export transaction and to use this analysis as a basis for support or denial of financing.
- **Environmental policy.** The Ex-Im Bank is the only ECA in the G-7 to commit systematically to publishing environmental monitoring reports, which includes carbon accounting of projects. In addition, the Ex-Im Bank faces competition from ECAs outside of the OECD, such as China, which tend to be less rigorous in their environmental requirements for financing than OECD countries.
- **Domestic content requirement.** In contrast to the Ex-Im Bank, the ECAs of other countries generally have lower domestic content requirements and some even have no domestic content requirements. ECAs of other countries have revised their content policies to reflect the changing nature of manufacturing, including the rise of global supply chains and the sourcing of product inputs from multiple countries. The Ex-Im Bank considers U.S. content to be a "proxy to evidence support for U.S. jobs" and seeks to balance the interests of multiple stakeholders through its content policy.[34]

Some U.S. business groups argue that certain Ex-Im Bank requirements are major constraints that limit the Ex-Im Bank's ability to compete with the ECAs of foreign countries.[35] They consider requirements for Ex-Im Bank support to be excessively burdensome and to detract from the ExIm Bank's core mission of boosting exports and supporting jobs.[36]

Another set of competitiveness issues focuses on the international rules governing official export credit activity. An increasingly important concern for U.S. policymakers is that some countries outside of the OECD, such as China, are becoming major providers of official export credit finance and may not be "playing by the rules." To the extent that the ECAs of China and other non-OECD countries provide financing on terms that are more advantageous than those allowed within the OECD Arrangement, the Ex-Im Bank and other OECD export credit agencies may find it difficult to compete with such export credit programs.

U.S. exporters and others have expressed doubts about the effectiveness of international efforts to stem officially subsidized trade financing. While the OECD Arrangement appears to be reducing most direct government subsidies for trade financing, a number of countries have found a way around the agreement, such as through market windows, that are not subject to the agreement. The agreement also has a number of limitations, including the difficulty of defining commercially viable projects, and the presence of an "escape clause" that allows countries to proceed with a tied aid offer, despite objections by other participants, if that country claims that the project is in its national interest. Moreover, the agreement contains no explicit enforcement mechanism. The effectiveness of the agreement also depends on the accuracy and openness of tied aid offers reported to the OECD, but the OECD does not confirm or verify the accuracy of the data provided by its members.[37]

Organizational Structure

Congress may examine the Ex-Im Bank within the context of debates about trade reorganization. There has been renewed interest on the part of the Obama Administration and Congress in reorganizing the trade policy structure of the federal government in order to enhance the effectiveness of U.S. trade promotion efforts, improve U.S. trade policy coordination, avoid duplication of functions and activities, and for other reasons. On January 13, 2012, President Obama asked Congress for authority to reorganize and consolidate the business- and trade-related functions of six federal entities into one department in an effort to streamline the federal government. In addition to the Ex-Im Bank, the other federal entities included in the proposal are the Department of Commerce, Overseas Private Investment Corporation (OPIC), Small Business Administration (SBA), Trade and Development Agency (TDA), and the U.S. Trade Representative (USTR).[38]

Some proponents of trade reorganization argue that consolidation of federal trade functions may increase the effectiveness of federal export promotion efforts and reduce government costs. Supporters maintain that consolidation would also provide a more streamlined rationale for U.S. export promotion services based on more clearly defined goals. For example, there may be concerns that the distribution of trade and investment financing across multiple different agencies (Ex-Im Bank, USDA, SBA, and OPIC) can lead to fragmentation and duplication of services and make it more difficult for U.S. businesses to access federal export assistance. On the other hand, critics contend that consolidation could result in the creation of a large federal bureaucracy, with little effect on the ability of the U.S. government to expand exports, or result in federal export assistance that is not responsive to the specific needs of certain exporters.

Some supporters of trade reorganization advocate for privatizing or terminating the functions of the Ex-Im Bank. Central premises behind this option may include the fact that the Bank is self-sustaining, which is seen as proof that there is no market failure; concerns that the Bank may compete with or crowd out private sector export financing activity; the notion that the private sector is more efficient and better suited than the federal government to conduct export financing; and the risks to U.S. taxpayers of Ex-Im Bank financing. Opponents contend that Ex-Im Bank activities, backed by the full faith and credit of the U.S. government, may make certain export transactions, such as those for major infrastructure projects, more commercially attractive or may give the Bank leverage to guarantee repayment in a way that is not available to the private sector. In addition, critics may contend that federal financing of exports is important in times of financial crisis and to combat growing official export credit support by other countries.

CONGRESSIONAL OUTLOOK

The 112th Congress considered several pieces of legislation to renew the Ex-Im Bank's authority (H.R. 2072, S. 1547, S.Amdt. 1836, and H.R. 4302), and ultimately passed H.R. 2072, which extends the Ex-Im Bank's authority through FY2014. Congressional interest in the Ex-Im Bank could continue to be high due to a number of factors:

- The changing export finance landscape has intensified congressional interest in the Ex-Im Bank. The international financial crisis and global economic downturn that began in 2007 led to a decline in private sector export finance and a greater demand from U.S. exporters for Ex-Im Bank assistance.

- The burgeoning of officially backed export finance being conducted by emerging market economies that are not a part of the OECD, including China, Brazil, and India, has increased demand for competitive financing from the Ex-Im Bank.
- The introduction of the NEI, and federal export promotion activities more broadly, have highlighted the role of the Ex-Im Bank as a tool for supporting U.S. jobs, contributing to U.S. economic recovery, and contributing to U.S. industrial competitiveness in the global market.
- The national debate about reducing the size of government and federal spending has stimulated debate about the appropriate organizational structure for U.S. government trade functions, including export financing function of the Ex-Im Bank.

End Notes

[1] A U.S. government corporation is a government agency established by Congress to provide market-oriented public services and to produce revenues that meet or approximate expenditures. For additional information, see CRS Report RL30365, *Federal Government Corporations: An Overview*, by Kevin R. Kosar.

[2] Certain provisions of Ex-Im Bank's Charter are codified at 12 U.S. Code Section 635 et. seq.

[3] The Federal Financing Bank (FFB) is a part of the Department of the Treasury and obtains its funds from regular Treasury issues.

[4] FFB, *Financial Statements*, multiple years, http://www.ustreas.gov/ffb/financial

[5] In previous years, appropriations legislation set a limit on the amount of offsetting collections in excess of obligations that could remain available for use in subsequent fiscal years.

[6] CRS Report RL30346, *Federal Credit Reform: Implementation of the Changed Budgetary Treatment of Direct Loans and Loan Guarantees*, by James M. Bickley.

[7] Ex-Im Bank website, http://www.exim.gov/.

[8] 12 U.S.C §635e.

[9] Ex-Im Bank, 2011 Annual Report, p. 4.

[10] Ex-Im Bank 2011 Annual Report.

[11] Ex-Im Bank defines infrastructure to include "the large physical networks necessary for the function of commerce (e.g., highways, railroads, power-generation plants, pipelines and radio-transmission systems)," "goods and services required to maintain the health, cultural and social standards of a country or state (e.g., education and healthcare equipment and services), [and] transportation vehicles, such as aircraft and locomotives, and equipment and services related to mining industries." Ex-Im Bank 2011 Annual Report, "Infrastructure" section.

[12] Ex-Im Bank 2011 Annual Report, "Key Industries" section.

[13] Ex-Im Bank, *The Charter of the Export-Import Bank of the United States*, as amended through P.L. 109-438, December 20, 2006, pp. 10-11.

[14] U.S. Code Title 12, Chapter 6a, Section 635(b)(1)(B)(ii).

[15] Ex-Im Bank, *The Charter of the Export-Import Bank of the United States*, as amended through P.L. 109-438, updated December 27, 2006, §2(b)(1)(E)(v).

[16] Ibid., §2(b)(1)(K).

[17] See CRS Report R41495, *U.S. Government Agencies Involved in Export Promotion: Overview and Issues for Congress*, coordinated by Shayerah Ilias.

[18] Office of the U.S. Trade Representative, *2012 Trade Policy Agenda and 2011 Annual Report*, March 2012, http://www.ustr.gov/about-us/press-office/reports-and-publications/2012-0.

[19] The Trade Promotion Coordinating Committee (TPCC), first established in May 1990 by President Bush during remarks on U.S. trade policies and U.S. companies involved in exporting, was enacted in statute by the Export Enhancement Act of 1992 (15 U.S.C. 4727).

[20] U.S. Congress, House Committee on Financial Services, Subcommittee on International Monetary Policy and Trade, *Statement for the Record from the Coalition for Employment through Exports*, 112th Cong., 1st sess., March 10, 2011.

[21] Ex-Im Bank's annual competitiveness report provides estimates of new MLT official export credit financing by ExIm Bank, the ECAs of the other G-7 countries (Canada, France, Germany, Italy, and the United Kingdom), and selected emerging economies (Brazil, China, and India).

[22] Stephen J. Ezell, *Understanding the Importance of Export Credit Financing to U.S. Companies*, The Information Technology & Innovation Foundation (ITIF), June 2011.

[23] Canada does not adhere to the home market rule. As such, it provides officially supported export financing for the sale of Bombardier aircraft in the United States.

[24] Ex-Im Bank, *Report to the U.S. Congress on Export Credit Competition and the Export-Import Bank of the United States, For the Period January 1, 2009 through December 31, 2009*, Washington, DC, June 2010.

[25] "Export Credit Pact Sought by U.S., China Would Replace OECD Guidelines," *Inside U.S. Trade's World Trade Online*, February 24, 2012. Doug Palmer, "U.S., China Agree to Negotiate Export Credit Deal," *Reuters*, April 14, 2012.

[26] The White House, "Remarks by the President on American Manufacturing," press release, February 17, 2012, http://www.whitehouse.gov/the-press-office/2012/02/17/remarks-president

[27] The White House, "President Obama Takes Actions to Promote American Manufacturing and http://www.whitehouse.gov/the-press-office/2012/02/17/president-

[28] "Ex-Im Financing for Foreign-Backed Sales in U.S. Hinges on Charter," *Inside U.S. Trade's World Trade Online*, February 24, 2012.

[29] Ex-Im Bank, *Report to the U.S. Congress on Export Credit Competition and the Export-Import Bank of the United States*, For the period January 1, 2010 through December 31, 2010, January 2010, p. 110. Sudeep Reddy, "U.S. Export Financing Challenges China," *The Wall Street Journal*, January 12, 2011.

[30] "White House Explores Financing Options, But Faces Obstacles," *Inside U.S. Trade's World Trade Online*, February 2, 2012.

[31] CRS analysis of data in Ex-Im Bank annual reports data.

[32] Ex-Im Bank annual reports.

[33] Jordan Jay Hillman, *The Export-Import Bank at Work: Promotional Financing in the Public Sector* (Westport, CT: Quorum Books, 1982), pp. 69 and 75.

[34] Ex-Im Bank 2011 annual competitiveness report.

[35] Matthew Schewel, "CEE Pushes for Ex-Im Changes in Next Year's Charter Reauthorization," *Inside U.S. Trade*, July 16, 2010.

[36] Hillman (1982), p. 58.

[37] U.S. General Accounting Office (now called the General Accountability Office), *Competitors' Tied Aid Practices Affect U.S. Exports*, GGD-94-81, May 1994, pp. 19-21.

[38] The White House, "Government Reorganization Fact Sheet," press release, January 13, 2012, http://www.whitehouse.gov/the-press-office/2012/01/13/government-reorganization-fact-sheet.

In: The Export-Import Bank of the United States   ISBN: 978-1-62618-709-2
Editor: Fraser M. Mulder   © 2013 Nova Science Publishers, Inc.

Chapter 2

REAUTHORIZATION OF THE EXPORT-IMPORT BANK: ISSUES AND POLICY OPTIONS FOR CONGRESS[*]

Shayerah Ilias

SUMMARY

The Export-Import Bank of the United States (Ex-Im Bank, EXIM Bank, or the Bank), a self-sustaining agency, is the official U.S. export credit agency (ECA). It operates under a renewable charter, the Export-Import Bank Act of 1945 (P.L. 79-173), as amended. Potential issues for Congress in examining the Ex-Im Bank's authority include the following:

- **The economic rationale for the Bank**, including the role of the federal government in export promotion and finance;
- **Specific Bank policies**, such as those relating to content, shipping, economic and environmental impact analysis, and tied aid, including how these policies balance U.S. export and other policy interests;
- **Statutory requirements directing the Ex-Im Bank to support certain types of exports**, such as exports of small businesses and "green" technology, including the tension that such requirements can create between desiring to support specific economic sectors and

---

[*] This is an edited, reformatted and augmented version of Congressional Research Service, Publication No. R41829, dated May 29, 2012.

allowing the Ex-Im Bank flexibility to fulfill its mission to support U.S. exports and jobs; and

- **International developments that may affect the Bank's work**, such as the growing role of emerging economies' ECAs and the sufficiency of the Organization for Economic Cooperation and Development (OECD) Arrangement on Officially Supported Export Credits to "level the playing field" for U.S. exporters.

Potential options for Congress include, but are not limited to, the following areas:

- **Structure of the Bank.** Congress could maintain the Ex-Im Bank as an independent agency, reorganize or privatize the functions of the Bank, or terminate the Bank.
- **Length of reauthorization.** Congress could extend the Bank's authority for a few years at a time (as in previous reauthorizations), for a longer period of time, or permanently reauthorize the Bank.
- **Bank's policies.** Congress could maintain the status quo, or revise the Bank's policies, such as those related to the requirements and limitations on the Ex-Im Bank's credit and insurance activities.
- **International ECA context.** Congress could seek to enhance international regulation of official export credit activity through the OECD or other mechanisms, or enhance the Ex-Im Bank's understanding of international export credit activity and trends.

Most recently, Congress passed H.R. 2072 to extend the Bank's authority through FY2014; previously, the Bank's authority was extended to May 31, 2012. H.R. 2072 also raises the Bank's lending authority incrementally from the previous $100 billion limit to $140 billion in FY2014, contingent on certain other requirements. In addition, H.R. 2072, among other things, includes provisions related to the Bank's domestic content policy and requirements to conduct international negotiations to reduce and eliminate official export credit activity. Prior to final action, the 112th Congress considered several other bills related to the Ex-Im Bank's authority.

INTRODUCTION

The Export-Import Bank of the United States (Ex-Im Bank, EXIM Bank, or the Bank) operates under a renewable charter, the Export-Import Bank Act of 1945 (P.L. 79-173), as amended. As part of its legislative responsibilities concerning the Ex-Im Bank, a central issue for Congress is whether to reauthorize the Bank's charter, and if so, for how long and under what terms. Congress's decisions on this issue could affect U.S. export promotion activities and U.S. industries whose exports are facilitated by the Bank's operations. Ex-Im Bank reauthorization emerged as a topic of debate in the 112th Congress, as the authority of the Bank would have expired unless extended by Congress. In 2006, Congress had extended the Bank's authority through September 30, 2011 (P.L. 109-438). Since then, Congress had extended the Bank's authority through appropriations vehicles, the latest of which had extended the Bank's authority through May 31, 2012 (P.L. 112-74). The 112th Congress considered several pieces of legislation related to Ex-Im Bank's authority, and ultimately passed a bill to extend the Ex-Im Bank's authority through FY2014 (H.R. 2072).

BACKGROUND

Overview of the Ex-Im Bank

The Ex-Im Bank is the official export credit agency (ECA) of the United States. The Bank was established in 1934 and became an independent agency in the executive branch in 1945. Its mandate is to support U.S. exports and the employment of U.S. workers. With respect to the ExIm Bank, Congress has an important role in reauthorization, appropriation, and oversight functions. The Ex-Im Bank uses its authority and resources to finance U.S. exports primarily in circumstances when alternative, private sector export financing may not be available or is prohibitively expensive or risky. It also may provide financing to support the competitiveness of U.S. exporters in circumstances when foreign governments extend export financing to their firms. The Ex-Im Bank's transactions are backed by the full faith and credit of the U.S. government. The Bank's charter requires that its financing have a reasonable assurance of repayment; directs the Bank to supplement, and not compete with, private capital; requires the Bank to notify Congress of proposed transactions above $100 million; and includes other limitations on the Bank's activities. Previously, the Bank's authority to lend, guarantee, and insure was statutorily limited to a total of $100 billion (P.L. 107-189). The recent Ex-Im Bank reauthorization bill passed by Congress (H.R. 2072) raises the authority incrementally to $140 billion in FY2014. Since its inception, the Bank estimates that it has supported more than $400 billion in U.S. exports. Its main programs to finance U.S. exports are direct loans, export credit guarantees, working capital guarantees, and export credit insurance. The Bank operates on a self-sustaining basis, using offsetting collections to fund administrative and program expenses.

Key Facts About Ex-Im Bank Programs

Products

- Direct loans: The Ex-Im Bank provides direct loans to foreign buyers of U.S. exports, generally for the purchase of capital-intensive goods such as commercial aircraft and mining equipment.
- Loan guarantees: The Ex-Im Bank guarantees a lender that, in the event of a payment default by the buyer, it will pay to the lender the outstanding principal and interest on the loan.
- Working capital guarantees: The Bank provides repayment guarantees to lenders (primarily commercial banks) on secured, short-term working capital loans made to qualified exporters with the objective of facilitating finance for businesses (generally, small businesses) that have exporting potential but need working capital funds.
- Insurance: The Ex-Im Bank provides insurance to U.S. exporters to protect them against losses should a foreign buyer or other foreign debtor default on the export contract for commercial or political reasons.
- Special financing programs: The Ex-Im Bank offers special financing programs that focus on a particular industry or financing technique, including aircraft finance, project finance, and supply chain finance.

Focus Areas

- Program-specific: The Ex-Im Bank focuses on increasing the number of small- and medium-sized enterprises (SMEs) using its products, supporting environmentally beneficial exports, and targeting business development to countries and in industries with high potential for U.S. export growth.
- Country-specific: The Ex-Im Bank operates in more than 160 countries around the world. Its current country priorities are Brazil, Colombia, India, Indonesia, Mexico, Nigeria, South Africa, Turkey, and Vietnam.
- Sector-specific: The Ex-Im Bank has identified industries with high potential for U.S. export growth: medical technology, construction, agricultural and mining equipment, and power generation (including renewable energy).

In addition, transportation—particularly large commercial aircraft—continues to be an important focal point.

Appropriations

The Ex-Im Bank has been "self-sustaining" for appropriations purposes since FY2008. It uses offsetting collections to cover its operations. Congress provides funding for the Ex-Im Bank's Office of Inspector General (OIG), and sets an upper limit on the level of the Bank's financial activities. The Ex-Im Bank receives a net appropriation of zero.

- FY2010: Congress appropriated $2.5 million for the OIG, and it authorized a limit of $58 million for the Bank's credit and insurance programs and a limit of $83.88 million for its administrative expenses (P.L. 111-117).
- FY2011: Congress authorized the Ex-Im Bank at FY2010 levels. It also included a rescission of $275 million of the unobligated balances available for funds appropriated under FY2009 Ex-Im Bank subsidy appropriations (P.L. 112-10).
- FY2012: Congress appropriated $4 million for the OIG, and it authorized a limit of $58 million for the Bank's credit and insurance programs and a limit of $89.9 million for its administrative expenses (P.L. 112-74).

Activity

- Large and small firms supported: By *dollar value* of transactions, large companies have received the majority of the Bank's support, whereas by *number of transactions*, small businesses have received the majority of its support.
- Level of activity: In FY2011, the Ex-Im Bank approved $33 billion in export financing (3,751 credit and insurance transactions), up from FY2010, when the Bank approved $24 billion in export financing (3,532 transactions).
- Exports supported: The Ex-Im Bank estimated that its activities supported about $41 billion in U.S. exports of goods and services in FY2011, up from $34 billion worth of exports in FY2010.
- Exposure: In FY2011, the Bank's total exposure stood at approximately $89 billion, up from approximately $75 billion FY2010.

Note: Summary of the Ex-Im Bank prepared by CRS, based on Ex-Im Bank annual reports from various years.

The Ex-Im Bank's Role in Promoting U.S. Exports

U.S. economic growth has traditionally been driven by consumption and borrowing, and historically there has been an undertow of belief that the U.S. economy does not need to rely on exports for economic growth. However, domestic consumption has been weak since the international financial crisis and global economic downturn in 2008. It also is a reflection of the fact that the United States is a relatively mature economy. Increasingly, the United States has turned to trade, in particular exports, as a means of growing the U.S. economy. The Ex-Im Bank, which is charged with supporting U.S. exports and jobs through export financing, is among the federal government agencies involved in promoting U.S. exports.[1] As such, the Ex-Im Bank is a key participant in President Obama's National Export Initiative (NEI), a strategy to double U.S. exports by 2015 to support U.S. employment. In September 2010, the Export Promotion Cabinet, a high-level cabinet created by Executive Order 13534, released a report containing recommendations for implementing the NEI. The Ex-Im Bank figures prominently in the report's recommendation to increase U.S. export financing. The Export Promotion Cabinet's report recommended the following actions in this priority area: (1) making more credit available, such as existing credit lines and new products; (2) expanding the eligibility criteria for providing credit and insurance to small- and medium-sized enterprises (SMEs); (3) focusing lending activities and outreach on priority international markets; (4) expanding and focusing outreach efforts on U.S. industries that are globally competitive and those that constitute underserved sectors of the economy; (5) increasing the number and scope of public-private partnerships that build awareness of export finance assistance and help to originate and underwrite transactions on behalf of the federal government; and (6) streamlining the application and review process of U.S. exporters applying for federal export credit and insurance.[2] Although the Ex-Im Bank is the official U.S. export credit agency, other agencies—the U.S. Department of Agriculture, Small Business Administration, and the Overseas Private Investment Corporation—also conduct export financing (see Table 1).

Ex-Im Bank Stakeholders

The Ex-Im Bank has a range of private and public stakeholders that have varying viewpoints and interests related to the Bank. They include the following:

- **U.S. businesses and their workers that receive Ex-Im Bank support**, which are arguably the most direct stakeholders of the Ex-Im Bank;
- **Indirect suppliers**, which are U.S. businesses (primarily SMEs) that supply goods and services to U.S. exporters and are considered by some groups to be "invisible exporters;"
- **Service exporters**, which have used Ex-Im Bank support less extensively than exporters of manufactured goods;
- **Import-sensitive U.S. industries**, such as steel, which may be adversely affected if Ex-Im Bank support for a particular export contract, such as for products used to build a steel mill in a foreign country, results in the foreign production of an exportable good that competes with U.S. products;
- **International buyers** of Ex-Im Bank-financed U.S. exports of goods and services, who are from developing countries and emerging markets. Ex-Im Bank products, such as direct loans, loan guarantees, and export insurance, may help to facilitate their purchases of U.S. exports of goods and services;
- **U.S. and international commercial lenders and insurers** that use Ex-Im Bank credit and insurance programs;[3]
- **State, county, and local nonprofit economic development organizations** with which the Ex-Im Bank collaborates to facilitate export opportunities;[4]
- **U.S. federal government agencies** with which the Ex-Im Bank collaborates on certain export-financing activities and specific programs and initiatives; and
- **Non-governmental organizations**, such as industry and trade associations, civil society advocacy groups, and public policy think tanks that represent an array of commercial, labor, environmental, and other policy interests.

International Export Credit Environment

The Ex-Im Bank was established at a time when private sector trade finance was limited. As international trade has grown, exporting financing has expanded. It is now a trillion-dollar market that supports approximately 10% of global trade.[5] It consists of private lenders and insurers, who operate commercially, and official export credit agencies (ECAs), which are backed by their governments. Private lenders and insurers conduct the majority of short-term export financing, whereas ECAs are more heavily involved in medium- and long-term export financing, including financing for complex, multi-billion dollar sales such as aircraft and infrastructure projects. The role of ECAs has become more prominent in recent years due to the international financial crisis and global economic downturn in 2008. With businesses facing difficulty accessing credit in the private sector, there has been a surge in demand for export credit and insurance from ECAs.

Table 1. U.S. Government Agencies that Conduct Export Financing

Federal Agency	Activities
Ex-Im Bank	Provides credit and insurance to support manufacturing and services exports, including for exports by small businesses
U.S. Department of Agriculture (USDA)	Conducts agricultural export financing
Small Business Administration (SBA)	Provides export financing for U.S. small businesses
Overseas Private Insurance Corporation (OPIC)	Provides credit and political risk insurance to support U.S. investments for projects in developing countries and emerging markets that may generate demand for U.S. exports

Source: CRS analysis.

Changing Composition of ECAs and Increasing Export Credit Competition

Since the Ex-Im Bank's inception in 1934, the process of globalization has introduced fundamental changes to the global economy and to the international export credit environment.

Traditionally, the United States and other developed countries have been the primary sources of world trade flows and ECA financing. For example, historically the G-7 countries have accounted for about 80% of global medium- to long-term export finance.[6]

As members of the Organization for Economic Cooperation and Development (OECD), these countries are party to the OECD Arrangement on Official Supported Export Credits (the "OECD Arrangement"), which is intended to ensure that exporting takes place on a level playing field (see text box, "International Disciplines on Export Credit Activity").

International Disciplines on Export Credit Activity[7]

Growing export credit competition has led to a strengthening of standards on official export credit activity. The international disciplines under which ECAs conduct their activities vary based on which organizations the country of the ECA is a member.

- Organization for Economic Cooperation and Development (OECD): The primary organization guiding and monitoring ECA activity is the OECD, which is composed of about 30 advanced industrialized economies, including the United States. The OECD Arrangement on Officially Supported Export Credits (the "OECD Arrangement"), created in 1978, established limitations on the terms and conditions for official export credit activity. It includes financial terms and conditions, such as down payments, repayment terms, interest rates, and country risk classifications; provisions on tied aid; notification procedures; and sector-specific terms and conditions, covering the export credits for ships, nuclear power plants, civil aircraft, renewable energies, and water projects. Military equipment, agricultural goods, and untied development aid are not covered by the agreement. The OECD lacks the authority to enforce compliance with its agreements, though members generally monitor compliance and raise concerns when members' policies and actions are viewed as violating the OECD Arrangement. The United States has been working through the OECD for decades to help level the playing field for U.S. exporters.
- World Trade Organization (WTO): The WTO, a multilateral organization for negotiating, governing, and enforcing international trade rules, plays a role in guiding export credit activity, but traditionally has deferred to the OECD. The WTO Agreement on Subsidies and Countervailing Measures (SCM) disciplines the use of subsidies, and it regulates the actions countries can take to counter the effects of these subsidies. The SCM Agreement language is interpreted to indicate that, for non-agricultural products, an export credit practice in conformity with the OECD Arrangement shall not be considered as an export subsidy prohibited by the SCM Agreement.[8]
- Berne Union: The Berne Union, an association for export credit and insurance globally, collects statistical data on the export credit activity of its members. It has 49 members that are major private creditors and insurers and ECAs.

Berne Union members span both advanced industrialized countries and emerging market countries. Berne Union members abide by a number of "guiding principles," which include supporting the stability and expansion of global trade, managing risks, practicing sound business practices, taking into account environmental and other considerations in activities, combating corruption, enhancing transparency, and fostering cooperation with other export trade and investment businesses. The Berne Union principles are not legally binding.[9]

Over the past couple of decades, economic changes associated with globalization have led to the rising wealth of emerging economies and their growing role in the global economy. Currently, a number of emerging market countries operate ECAs.[10] Rising economic powers, such as China, India, and Brazil, are not members of the OECD (though they may have observer status during some OECD meetings and the OECD has offered them "enhanced engagement" with a view toward possible accession). As non-member economies, China, India, and Brazil are not party to the OECD Arrangement, and their export credit financing activities may not comply with international standards.[11] For example, they may offer below-market and concessionary financing alternatives with which it is difficult for ECAs of OECD members to compete. The growing number of players and volumes of export credit activity in the international export finance market has resulted in greater and varied competition for U.S. exporters, both from developed countries and from rising economic powers as they move up the value chain.[12] In terms of developed countries, although certain types of competition between developed country ECAs that were prevalent in the 1970s and 1980s have been reduced, new forms of competition have emerged. For example, for about 30 years, the ECAs of developed countries generally have not offered officially supported financing for exports to other developed countries. With respect to the aircraft sector, the Ex-Im Bank and the ECAs of the United Kingdom, France, Spain, and Germany (which provide financing to Airbus) have agreed to an informal "home market rule," which limits access to officially supported export financing for the purchase of aircraft in their own domestic market and in each other's "home markets." The competitive landscape appears to be changing, however. Canada currently does not recognize the home market rule, and the Canadian aircraft manufacturer Bombardier, which is supported by Canada's official ECA, has recently entered the large civil aircraft market. This trend is also emerging in other sectors, such as in green energy projects. For instance, the Japanese ECA reportedly recently announced that it was prepared to support its companies on projects in the United States, including the Florida high speed rail project.[13] In terms of emerging economies, the increasing volumes of their official export credit activity that fall outside of the OECD Arrangement have raised concerns among OECD members about how level the playing field is for their exporters. According to the Ex-Im Bank, non-OECD countries are expected to continue "expanding their market share by using exceptional financing methods, that comport with WTO provisions, but that are outside of the purview of the OECD rules, further expanding the scope of unregulated financing vis-à-vis constant volumes of OECD Arrangement-compliant activity."[14] Officially subsidized export credit activity by emerging economies may increase in strategic markets, such as oil and gas, renewable energy, and natural resources extraction.[15] For instance, Chinese ECAs "have shown strong signs of growing usage of export credits for export promotion purposes, especially in Africa, where they were offering preferential loans either in exchange for much needed resources (e.g., oil) or low cost loans on very extended repayment terms on projects in order to gain market share."[16] The rise of emerging economies as financing competitors has renewed concerns about a new "race to the bottom."

Growth in Publicly Backed Export Credit Support

Comprehensive data on the export finance activities of ECAs are limited and sometimes not publicly available. It also can be difficult to compare activity across ECAs, because the characteristics of the ECAs and the types of transactions may vary. The OECD and Berne Union are engaged in efforts to enhance international export credit data.[17] What follows are some data that may provide an indication of the levels of international export credit activity.

- In 2010, Berne Union members (both public and private) provided $1.4 trillion in credit and investment insurance support, covering more than 10% of the value of international trade transactions with their export credit support.[18] Berne Union members generally cover the more risky transactions in which exporters and lenders decide to take insurance to mitigate the risks of trading.

- The Ex-Im Bank's annual competitiveness report provides estimates of new medium- and long-term (MLT) official export credit financing by the Ex-Im Bank, the ECAs of the other G-7 countries, and selected emerging economies In 2010, new MLT official export credit financing by the G-7 ECAs totaled $65.4 billion. The United States represented 20% of total new MLT financing by the G7 countries. In comparison to the G-7, the emerging economies of Brazil, China, and India conducted a total of $72.7 billion in new MLT financing in 2010, surpassing that of the G-7 (see Table 2).

Table 2. Selected ECAs: New Medium- to Long-Term Official Export Credit Volumes (Billions of U.S. dollars)

Country	ECAs			Year	
G-7 ECAs (OECD Members)		2007	2008	2009	2010
Canada	Export Development Canada (EDC)	0.5	1.5	2.0	2.5
France	Compagnie Française d'Assurance pour le Commerce Extérieur (COFACE)	10.1	8.6	17.8	17.4
Germany	Euler Hermes	8.9	10.8	12.9	22.5
Italy	S.p.A. Servizi Assicurativi del Commercio Estero (SACE)	3.5	7.6	8.2	5.3
Japan	Japan Bank for International Cooperation (JBIC), Nippon Export and Investment Insurance (NEXI)	1.8	1.5	2.7	2.9
United Kingdom	Export Credits Guarantee Department (ECGD)	0.4	0.8	1.4	1.9
United States	Export-Import Bank of the United States (Ex-Im Bank)	8.2	11.0	17.0	13.0
Total G-7 Volumes		33.4	41.8	62.0	65.4
Selected Emerging Market Countries					
Brazil	Brazilian Development Bank (BNDES), Seguradora Brasileira Crédito à Exportação (SBCE)	7.0	7.6	10.5	18.2
China	Export-Import Bank of China, Sinosure, China Development Bank (CDB)	33.0	52.0	51.1	45.0
India	Export-Import Bank of India, Export Credit Guarantee Corporation of India (ECGC)	8.5	8.7	7.3	9.5
Total Brazil, China, and India Volumes		48.5	68.3	68.9	72.7

Source: Data on export credit volumes from the Ex-Im Bank, Report to the U.S. Congress on Export Credit Competition and the Export-Import Bank of the United States, For the Period January 1, 2010 through December 31, 2010, Washington, DC, June 2011.

Notes: The Ex-Im Bank Competitiveness Report states that, for the G-7 countries, the Bank attempted to differentiate the standard, officially supported export credits that are regulated by the OECD Arrangement and export credits that are not subject to the OECD Arrangement. The Competitiveness Report also states that data on export credit volumes for Brazil, China, and India are approximations of activity based on available information and may be overstated due to the analytic assumptions used by the Bank.

Characteristics of ECAs

ECAs vary widely in a number of characteristics, including

- **Mandates:** Some ECAs focus primarily on advancing commercial objectives, such as facilitating exports, business-to-business trade, and filling in the gaps in the private sector export credit activity. A number of the G-7 ECAs have "lender of last resort" approaches (i.e., to provide finance where private sector finance is not available and to charge fees for their services), including those of the United States, the United Kingdom, France, Germany, and Japan.

  Canada's ECA takes a more expansive view of commercial interests than some other ECAs, and focuses on supporting Canadian exports and developing Canada's trade capacity both directly and indirectly. Other ECAs, generally in emerging markets, focus primarily on advancing economic development objectives, such as increasing living standards, and boosting the competitiveness of their firms.[19]

- **Products:** ECAs offer a range of products that may include direct loans, guarantees, working capital loans, and tied aid. These products can vary by short, medium, and long terms.

  Some ECAs offer credit and insurance products directed toward supporting exports, whereas others focus on supporting both exports and overseas investment.

  In the United States, the Ex-Im Bank provides credit and insurance to support exports, whereas the Overseas Private Investment Corporation (OPIC), another U.S. agency, provides political risk insurance to support overseas investment. In several other countries, such as Japan and Canada, the same entity (i.e., JBIC and EDC, respectively) conducts both export and investment support and others forms of export assistance.

- **Policies:** Some ECAs determine whether or not to support export contracts based on an array of criteria, such as the economic and environmental impact of the proposed transactions or the strategic implications of the financing.

  Compared with other ECAs (both OECD member and non-member), the Ex-Im Bank's policies for extending support tend to be more stringent.

ISSUES FOR CONGRESS

Congressional examination of the Ex-Im Bank for reauthorization generally has included examining the Bank's effectiveness and efficiency of the Bank in supporting exports broadly and in particular sectors, specific Bank policies, and its competitiveness in comparison to foreign ECAs. Many of the issues discussed below arise from congressional statutes and mandates incorporated into the Ex-Im Bank's charter.

The Bank's Mission

Over time, Congress has debated the acceptability of federal support of private firms to export, with some viewing federal export financing as a form of targeted favoritism, or "corporate welfare," and others considering it to be acceptable for certain large-scale or high-cost capital-intensive projects where private financing is unavailable. Advocates of the Ex-Im Bank's credit and insurance programs argue that such efforts are critical in addressing market failures (such as imperfect information and barriers to entry) and countering foreign governments' export financing efforts. Others, including some economists, hold that such programs merely shift production among sectors within the economy and do not permanently add to the overall level of a nation's exports, which they argue is influenced by a combination of domestic macroeconomic factors and global economic developments in the long run. Some also may question whether this form of government intervention has crowded out private sector financing.

A long-standing concern about the Ex-Im Bank centers on the composition of firms benefiting from Ex-Im Bank services. Large firms account for about 80% of the *dollar value* of the Ex-Im Bank's credit and insurance authorizations and small firms account for about 20%. In contrast, small firms account for about 80% of the *number* of the Ex-Im Bank's credit and insurance transactions, whereas large firms account for about 20%. Supporters note that the Ex-Im Bank's mission is to support U.S. businesses of all sizes and that the Bank places special emphasis on supporting the exports of small businesses. Some supporters argue that focusing on the dollar value of Ex-Im Bank support to small businesses may be misleading because the larger size of corporations naturally results in a scale of business that requires larger volumes of support.

Some supporters also contend that Ex-Im Bank data do not reflect all of the small businesses that benefit from Ex-Im Bank services, such as "invisible" exporters who provide goods and services used by other companies that directly export. For example, one study identified more than 33,000 SMEs that supplied manufactured parts or services to five larger companies (General Electric, Boeing, Case New Holland, Siemens Power Corporation, and Bechtel) that use Ex-Im Bank financing. According to the study, the SMEs identified constitute a representative sample of those SMEs that serve as primary exporters for the larger "exporters of record."[20]

Limit on Outstanding Aggregate Credit and Insurance Authority

Congress sets limitations on the aggregate amounts of loan, guarantees, and insurance that the ExIm Bank can have outstanding at any one time (oftentimes referred to as the Ex-Im Bank's exposure cap/ceiling/limit).[21] The outstanding principal amount of all loans made, guaranteed, or insured by the Ex-Im Bank is charged at the full value against the limitation.

The Ex-Im Bank initially was capitalized with a stock of $1 billion in 1934. When Congress established the Ex-Im Bank as an independent agency in 1945, it authorized a limit on the Ex-Im Bank's outstanding aggregate credit and insurance authority that was no greater than three and one-half times the Bank's authorized stock of $1 billion. In 1951, Congress changed the statutory formula to four and one-half times the authorized stock. In 1954, Congress changed the outstanding limit from a formula calculation to $5 billion, and since then, has periodically enacted legislation that has increased the Bank's outstanding limitation (see Table 3).

H.R. 2072, the most recent Ex-Im Bank reauthorization bill passed by Congress, increases the Bank's exposure cap incrementally from the previous limitation of $100 billion (authorized under P.L. 107-189). H.R. 2072 increases the Bank's exposure cap to $120 billion in FY2012, $130 billion in FY2013, and $140 billion in FY2014, with the increase in the exposure cap for FY2013 and FY2014 contingent on the Bank maintaining a default rate of less than 2% and on meeting various reporting requirements.

At the end of FY2011, the Ex-Im Bank's exposure level was about $89 billion. Some U.S. businesses are concerned that the Ex-Im Bank may reach its exposure ceiling soon if it is not raised, which may adversely affect the Bank's ability finance large export transactions.[22]

Given that the Ex-Im Bank's credit and insurance transactions are backed by the full faith and credit of the U.S. government, the Ex-Im Bank's exposure cap can be viewed as the maximum amount for which U.S. taxpayers may be liable if the Bank's portfolio experiences severe losses. To date, the Ex-Im Bank's loan loss rate has been low historically, at approximately 1.5%.[23] Some opponents express concern about the potential burden to taxpayers imposed by the Bank's activities. Some argue that risks to the Bank's portfolio have increased with the global financial crisis and the Eurozone debt crisis. Supporters counter that the Ex-Im Bank is a self-sustaining agency; its charter requires a reasonable assurance of repayment for all credit authorizations; and that the Bank monitors credit and other risks in its portfolio.[24]

Table 3. Legislative Changes to the Export-Import Bank's Limit on Outstanding Aggregate Credit and Insurance Authority

Year	Legislation	New Limit Resulting from Legislation
1945	P.L. 79-173	Three and one-half times the authorized stock of $1 billion
1951	P.L. 82-158	Four and one-half times the authorized stock of $1 billion
1954	P.L. 83-570	$5 billion
1958	P.L. 85-424	$7 billion
1963	P.L. 88-101	$9 billion
1968	P.L. 90-267	$13.5 billion
1971	P.L. 92-126	$20 billion
1975	P.L. 93-646	$25 billion
1978	P.L. 95-630	$40 billion
1992	P.L. 102-429	$75 billion
2002	P.L. 107-189	Incremental increases in limit to $100 billion[a]
2012	H.R. 2072	Incremental increases in limit to $140 billion, contingent on certain requirements[a]

Source: U.S. Code notes; Lexis Nexis; and Jordan Jay Hillman, *The Export-Import Bank at Work* (Westport 1982).

[a] The Export-Import Bank Reauthorization Act of 2002 (P.L. 107-189) increased the Bank's exposure cap to $80 billion in FY2002, $85 billion in FY2003, $90 billion in FY2004, $95 billion in FY2005, and $100 billion in FY2006.

[b] The Export-Import Bank Reauthorization Act of 2012 (H.R. 2072) increases the Bank's exposure cap to $120 billion in FY2012, $130 billion in FY2013, and $140 billion in FY2014—with the increase in lending authority for FY2013 and FY2014 contingent on the Bank maintaining a "default rate" of less than 2% and on submitting various reports.

National Content

The OECD Arrangement does not contain specific guidelines regarding content requirements, which relate to the amount of domestic and foreign content (e.g., labor, materials, and overhead costs) associated with the production of an export. Each ECA generally establishes its own guidelines in this area, and these guidelines tend to vary among ECAs (see Table 4).

Table 4. Foreign Content Requirements of Selected Country ECAs

	Maximum Allowable Foreign Content to Receive
Country	Full Medium- and Long-Term Financing
Australia	15%
Canada	Support will be given if the transaction benefits national interest
France	40%; however, may allow more foreign content in transactions that advance strategic/national interests.
Germany	30% combined local and foreign (non-domestic) content; however may allow more non-domestic content in transactions that advance strategic/national interests
Italy	Support will be given if the transaction benefits national interest
Japan	70%; however, foreign content may be higher on a case-by-case basis
United States	15%
United Kingdom	80%; however, may allow more foreign content in transactions that advance strategic/national interests.

Sources: Ex-Im Bank, Report to the U.S. Congress on Export Credit Competition and the Export-Import Bank of the United States, For the Period January 1, 2009 through December 31, 2009, Washington, DC, June 2010; meeting with Ex-Im Bank officials, May 5, 2011; House Committee on Financial Services, Subcommittee on International Monetary Policy and Trade, The Role of the Ex-Im Bank in U.S. Competitiveness and Job Creation, opening statement by Chairman Gary Miller, 112th Cong., 1st sess., March 10, 2011; OECD, Export Credit Financing Systems in OECD Member Countries and Non-Member Economies, May 1, 2008.

Notes: These reported data on foreign content requirements should not be considered definitive; rather, these data are intended to give an idea of the different types of content requirements that foreign ECAs may employ. ECAs may not apply their content requirements on an absolute basis, and may consider requests for export financing on a case-by-case basis. They may apply flexibility to their content rules, for example, flexibility in terms of definition, percentage of foreign content, or interpretation of national benefit.

The Ex-Im Bank's content policy limits its support, for all medium- and long-term transactions, to the lesser of (1) 85% of the value of all goods and services contained within a U.S. supply contract or (2) 100% of the U.S. content of an export contract. In effect, the Ex-Im Bank has a foreign content allowance of 15%; if the foreign content exceeds 15%, the Bank's support would be reduced.[25]

The Ex-Im Bank's content policy seeks to ensure that its export financing targets the U.S. content directly associated with goods and services produced in the United States. The Ex-Im Bank considers U.S. content to be "a proxy to evidence support for U.S. jobs." The policy is intended to encourage U.S. companies to maximize their sourcing of U.S. content. However, the Ex-Im Bank recognizes that U.S. export contracts may contain goods and services that are foreign-originated, and it allows financing support for such contracts, subject to certain restrictions and limitations. According to the Ex-Im Bank, its policy "reflects a concerted attempt to balance the interests of multiple stakeholders."[26]

Changing International Perspectives on National Content

Traditionally, ECAs have linked their support for exports with national content. For some countries, exports of manufactured goods have typically accounted for a significant portion of their gross domestic product and economic growth. However, a number of ECAs have been re-evaluating their national content models in light of changes in the global economy. Over the past several decades, the process of globalization has led to the rise of global supply chains. Communication, transportation, and other technology advances enable firms to break up the production process into discrete steps and to manufacture goods and inputs in different locations to be globally competitive. Consequently, manufacturing and production have become transnational.

Given the changing nature of the global business environment, many ECAs have been reducing national content requirements. In the early 2000s, the majority of ECAs had requirements for 70%-100% national content, with a few ECAs permitting national content of 50%. In comparison, fewer ECAs currently have national content requirements of higher than 80%. Some, like Canada's official ECA, have no fixed requirement, whereas the U.S. Ex-Im Bank has an 85% requirement. Most ECAs now have fixed maximum allowances of foreign content of between 30% and 50%.

Some ECAs have eliminated national content rules in favor of assessing export contracts on the basis of their contribution to the "national interests" of the country. ECAs may evaluate transactions on a case-by-case basis, allowing them flexibility in supporting export contracts, possibly choosing to support deals with especially high foreign content in excess of their typical limit if they deem such transactions to be in the national interest. In some cases, ECAs may require higher national content if a particular transaction is considered to be especially risky. Some ECAs have been changing their definitions of what constitutes national content. In addition to accounting for direct exports of goods and services, they may also consider trade and investment that both directly and indirectly enhance the national interest. For instance, some ECAs may support exports by foreign subsidiaries of their national exporters. Such re-interpretations may be geared toward increasing the competitiveness of national companies in the global economy.

Canada's content rules are among the most flexible of ECAs. The mandate of Export Development Canada (EDC), Canada's ECA, is "to support and develop, directly or indirectly, Canada's export trade and Canadian capacity to engage in that trade as well as respond to international business opportunities." When determining whether to participate in a transaction, EDC considers the transaction's "potential benefit to Canada." It takes into account factors such as the transactions' effect on Canadian gross domestic product; research and development spending in Canada; possibility of increased access to global markets or integration in a key supply chain; employment impact; benefit to SMEs; the destination market for transaction (developed or developing); support of new technology or new product; positive environmental impact; and dividends, royalties, and licensing fees.

Sources: Berne Union, *Berne Union 2008*, pp. 29-31, http://www.berneunion. org.uk/pdf/Berne%20Union%20Yearbook%202008.pdf.
Export Development Canada (EDC), "Canadian Benefits," http://www.edc.ca /english/corporate_canadian_benefits.htm.

Given the proliferation of global supply chains, many U.S. businesses have been supportive of introducing additional flexibility in the Ex-Im Bank's content requirements. For example, the Coalition for Employment for Exports, an advocacy group composed of exporters, banks, and trade associations, has recommended that the Ex-Im Bank lower its domestic content requirement to

70% (i.e., the foreign content limit would be 30%); expand the definition of content to include "R&D, project and global supply chain management, and other elements" that reflect the value of the U.S. innovation economy; and to establish a "pilot program" whereby the Bank could support exports on a national interest benefit, which would allow the Bank to support exports that generate benefits to the U.S. economy "that are not otherwise captured by exclusive focus on the domestic manufactured content requirement."[27] Other industry proposals include recommending that the Ex-Im Bank lower U.S. content requirements for full financing to match the average among OECD countries or that the Ex-Im Bank adopt a policy similar to the European Union ECAs and "automatically cover non-U.S. content for U.S. FTA [free trade agreement] partners who offer reciprocity for U.S. content under their export credit agencies."[28]

However, labor groups tend to be concerned about the impact that lowering national content requirements may have on employment in the home country. There is concern that reducing these requirements may result in an outsourcing of labor to other countries. Others argue that such requirements may induce firms to use other ECAs for alternative sources of financing, which may cause them to shift production overseas.

Support for Services Exports

The Ex-Im Bank offers limited export credit and insurance to support exports of U.S. services. During the 2008-2010 period, the Ex-Im Bank reported that it provided financing for over $8 billion of U.S. services exports, comprising about one-tenth of the total export value estimated to be supported by the Ex-Im Bank during this time period.[29] The Ex-Im Bank's level of support for services exports is partly a function of the Bank's content rules, according to U.S. businesses. Some argue that the Bank's definition of national content does not take into account "the high value U.S. jobs in R&D [research and development], supply chain management, software design engineering, business development, and marketing, IP [intellectual property] support, branding, and profit."[30] Business groups contend that the Ex-Im Bank should target the services industries more given that services constitute the fastest growing sector of the U.S. economy.

There has been a broader recognition in the federal government that "traditional advocacy and trade promotion program efforts may overlook services." As part of implementing the NEI, the Export Promotion Cabinet recommends building on the activities and initiatives outlined in the other priority areas with an enhanced focus on services; ensuring better data and measurement of the services economy to help inform policy decisions more adequately; continuing to assess and focus on supporting services exports in key sectors and markets; and conducting better coordination of services export promotion efforts.[31]

Co-Financing

The Ex-Im Bank introduced the co-financing program in 2001. Co-financing arrangements enable export credit financing from multiple ECAs. They allow goods and services from two or more countries to be marketed to a buyer under a single ECA financing package. According to U.S. exporters and lenders, co-financing arrangements allow the Ex-Im Bank to participate with other ECAs on the non-U.S. content portion of an export contract. Otherwise, the Ex-Im Bank would be limited to supporting the U.S. portion of the export contract and face the risk of the U.S. exporter not winning the sale because the ECA supported portion was insufficient or the terms and conditions were disadvantageous. In 2010, the Ex-Im Bank conducted 34 co-financing transactions totaling $6.5 billion. About 98% of the volume of Ex-Im Bank co-financing transactions involved aircraft. The Bank states that, in most aircraft transactions, without co-financing, the exporter would not have been able to offer the maximum 85% support to its customers in one financing package.[32]

Shipping

The Ex-Im Bank's shipping policy is based on Public Resolution 17 (PR-17, approved March 26, 1934, by the 73rd Congress), whose purpose is to "support the U.S. strategic objective of maintaining a merchant marine sufficient to carry a substantial portion of its waterborne export and import foreign commerce."[33] Under the Ex-Im Bank's shipping policy, certain products supported by the Ex-Im Bank must be transported exclusively on U.S. vessels. Transactions subject to the Ex-Im Bank shipping requirement include direct loans of any amount, guarantees above $20 million, and products with repayment periods of more than seven years. Under limited conditions, a waiver on this requirement may be granted on a case-by-case basis by the U.S. Maritime Administration (MARAD).

Supporters contend that maintaining U.S. flag vessels is "critical to U.S. national security" and "essential to maintaining a commercial U.S.-flag merchant marine."[34] They argue that, from a budgetary standpoint, cargo preference is a "highly cost efficient way" to support a privately owned U.S.-

flag commercial fleet. Because the goods will be shipped regardless of which ship carries them, and therefore the cost will be incurred regardless, "requiring that some of the cargoes be shipped on U.S.-flag vessels leverages that basic transportation expense to provide other benefits to the nation at a fraction of direct cost purchase." The concern under this view is that otherwise, the U.S. government would have to "duplicate sealift capacity at enormous expense with government-owned vessels."[35] These merchant U.S.-flag vessels are then available to transport U.S. troops and military equipment. Proponents also argue that the cargo preference requirements help to support the U.S. shipping industry and the employment of shipboard crew.

Critics of the shipping policy argue that "both U.S. strategic requirements and the global shipping market have changed dramatically."[36] U.S. business groups contend that the Ex-Im Bank's shipping requirements can make U.S. goods less competitive relative to foreign goods for a host of reasons. Most other ECAs do not have such cargo preference requirements. Of the other G-7 ECAs, only the ECAs of France and Italy have cargo preference requirements similar to those of the Ex-Im Bank. In addition, U.S.-flagged shippers generally charge higher rates. There may also be capacity constraints because there are a limited number of U.S. bulk cargo carriers. According to lenders and exporters, the higher rates and the route scheduling challenges associated with shipping with U.S.-flagged vessels can make it difficult for them to use Ex-Im Bank support. For example, in one transaction with the Ex-Im Bank, the cost of U.S. shipping reportedly was five times the cost of non-U.S. shipping.[37] Some critics further argue that, in some instances, the increased cost of an export contract associated with the shipping requirement may be the only reason why the U.S. exporter loses business to a foreign competitor. In addition, some businesses argue that obtaining a waiver from MARAD can be time-consuming, burdensome, and complex.

Economic and Environmental Impact Analysis

Congress requires the Bank to take into account the possible economic and environmental implications of proposed Ex-Im Bank support for certain export transactions.

- **Economic considerations:** Congress requires that Ex-Im Bank-financed exports have no adverse effects on U.S. industry and employment. The Bank must conduct an economic impact assessment on all transactions of more than $10 million of Ex-Im Bank financing or transactions that are subject to specific trade measures (such as anti-dumping and countervailing duties). Chiefly, the Ex-Im Bank may not support projects that enable foreign production of an exportable good that would compete with U.S. production of the same, or a similar, good and that would cause "substantial injury" to U.S. producers. The Ex-Im Bank also may not support projects that result in the foreign production of a good that is substantially the same as a good subject to specified U.S. trade measures such as anti-dumping or countervailing duty investigations.

- **Environmental considerations:** The Ex-Im Bank's charter authorizes the Bank to grant or withhold financing support after taking into account the potential beneficial and adverse environmental effects of goods and services for which ExIm Bank direct lending and guarantee support is requested. The Bank must conduct an environmental review on all transactions greater than $10 million.

Some U.S. exporters are concerned that the Ex-Im Bank's economic and environmental impact policies may be too overly burdensome and detract from the Ex-Im Bank's core mission to support U.S. exports and jobs. For example, some might argue that situations in which the Ex-Im Bank denies financing for projects that do not meet environmental requirements are contrary to the Ex-Im Bank's mission because denial of such financing may result in lost export and employment opportunities. According to the Ex-Im Bank's 2011 Competitiveness Report, these policies can lower its competitiveness. Among the G-7 ECAs, the Ex-Im Bank is the only ECA that is required to use an economic impact analysis to weigh the costs and benefits of supporting an export. Foreign ECAs do not tend to take environmental standards into consideration to the extent that the United States does when determining whether to support a transaction. Currently, the Ex-Im Bank is the only ECA in the G-7 to commit systematically to publishing environmental monitoring reports, which includes carbon accounting of projects. In addition, the Ex-Im Bank faces competition from ECAs outside of the OECD, such as those from China, that tend to be less rigorous in their environmental requirements for financing than OECD countries. However, import-sensitive U.S. businesses, labor groups, environmental groups, and other stakeholders contend that the Bank must balance U.S. exporting interests with other policy considerations.

In recent months, debate about the economic impact of Ex-Im Bank activities has been driven in part by a charge by Delta Airlines and other U.S.

airlines, led by the Air Transport Association of America (ATAA), that Ex-Im Bank financing for Boeing aircraft exports to India and other countries has led to an oversupply of airline seats that has had an adverse effect on their businesses. The group also has charged that the Ex-Im Bank's economic impact analysis procedures are inconsistent with the Bank's charter. Delta and these other airlines have filed a legal challenge against the Ex-Im Bank seeking an injunction on Ex-Im Bank loan guarantees to Air India. Following a federal judge's denial for a preliminary injunction that would stop Ex-Im Bank financing of Boeing exports to India, the airlines filed a motion on February 1, 2012, for a judgment on the merits of the case, which is pending in the U.S. District Court for the District of Columbia.[38]

Tied Aid

As part of its direct lending program, the Bank has a Tied Aid Capital Projects Fund (TACPF), often referred to as the tied aid "war chest," that it uses to counter specific projects that are receiving foreign officially subsidized export financing, or "concessional" below-market financing. Tied aid may be used to counter attempts by foreign governments to sway purchases in favor of their exporters solely on the basis of subsidized financing rather than on market conditions (price, quality, etc.).

The United States does tie substantial amounts of its agricultural and military aid to U.S. goods, but it has generally avoided using such financing to promote U.S. capital goods exports. The tied aid war chest stands at about $171 million.[39] Funds for the tied aid war chest are available to the Bank from the Treasury Department and are subtracted from the Bank's direct credit resources. Applications for the tied aid fund are subject to review by the Treasury Department.

According to the 2011 Ex-Im Bank Competitiveness Report, some U.S. exporters and lenders believe that the Ex-Im Bank's tied aid policies may place them at a competitive disadvantage.

U.S. exporters have expressed concern that increased tied aid activity by other countries, coupled with the more flexible tied aid rules of other ECAs, has threatened certain U.S. exporter sales prospects. Some groups argue that the tied aid war chest funds should be increased and that the Ex-Im Bank should have more flexibility and authority in initiating tied aid to compete with foreign ECAs for export contracts.

International Tied Aid Activity and Trends

The United States has worked through the OECD for many years to reduce tied aid competition. In 2010, tied aid activity (as reported to the OECD) stood at $5.8 billion, up from $4.6 billion in 2009. Japan accounted for nearly half of the tied aid activity by value. Other significant sources of tied aid were Spain, Korea, and France. The East Asia and Pacific region was the primary recipient of tied aid. Tied aid was generally used for transport and storage, education, health and water supply, and sanitation projects, which primarily tend to be non-commercially viable projects. However, the use of concessional financing by some foreign countries has been increasing in recent years. Countries have used tied aid to establish a market presence in countries for strategic industries such as renewable energy. A growing number of emerging economies that are outside of the OECD, such as China, have been conducting tied aid transactions.

In 2011, the Ex-Im Bank agreed to a $477 million financing deal to match China's financing terms in order to entice the Pakistani government to buy 150 General Electric Company locomotives. China, which is not a member of the OECD, offered financing terms for the export of Chinese railcars to Pakistan that were cheaper than those allowed by the OECD Arrangement on Export Credits. The matching deal required the Ex-Im Bank to work with the OECD. The deal has not been finalized.

Sources: Ex-Im Bank, Report to the U.S. Congress on Export Credit Competition and the Export-Import Bank of the United States, For the Period January 1, 2010 through December 31, 2010, Washington, DC, June 2011. Sudeep Reddy, "U.S. Export Financing Challenges China," The Wall Street Journal, January 12, 2011.

Congressional Mandates on Targeting Ex-Im Bank Activity to Specific Sectors

Certain congressional directives in the Ex-Im Bank's charter and appropriations language require the Ex-Im Bank to support exports in specific sectors, namely the exports of small businesses and exports of "green" technologies. The Bank's charter requires it to make available not less than 20% of its aggregate loan, guarantee, and insurance authority to directly finance exports by small businesses. The charter also requires the Bank to promote the export of goods and services related to renewable energy sources; in recent years, appropriations language has further specified that the Bank should make available not less than 10% of its aggregate credit and insurance authority for the financing of exports of renewable energy technologies or energy efficient end-use technologies.

Supporters of such congressional mandates contend that they enable the Ex-Im Bank to support strategic, high-growth sectors in the U.S. economy and, as in the case of SMEs, to support U.S. exporters that need the financing assistance the most. Critics contend that such policies essentially are a mechanism whereby the federal government determines "winners and losers" in the market, maintaining that such action can lead to economic distortions and harm other productive U.S. firms. Although such requirements give Congress a greater role in guiding the Ex-Im Bank's activities, some stakeholders contend that they may constrain the activities of the Bank and obscure its mission to support U.S. exports and employment broadly speaking. They also argue that the Ex-Im Bank's budget is inadequate to support multiple missions.

Some stakeholders express concern that such mandates may not be feasible to achieve. Although the Ex-Im Bank has met the small business target in recent years, its authorizations of "green" exports, while increasing, has been less than 2% of its total annual authorizations. In congressional testimony, Ex-Im Bank President and Chairman Hochberg stated,

> While Ex-Im understands and appreciates the legislative goal that 10% of its authorizations should support environmentally-beneficial exports, this may be a challenging target to achieve. Given that Ex-Im's expected FY2010 authorizations of about $25 billion and that the total value of renewable energy exports from the United States is about $2 billion, Ex-Im could support virtually all renewable exports and still not reach the 10% goal. That said, the Bank remains committed to expanding its support of environmental exports.[40]

International Context

Stakeholders have debated whether the OECD Arrangement on Officially Supported Export Credits is effective in leveling the playing field for exporters in the current trading environment. By some estimates, the OECD Arrangement has saved U.S. taxpayers $800 million annually. According to the Office of the U.S. Trade Representative, the minimum interest rate rules set by the OECD Arrangement limit subsidized export financing and reduce competition based on below-cost interest rates and long repayment terms by ECAs. The minimum exposure fees for country risks also reduce costs. In addition, the further leveling of the playing field created by the OECD tied aid disciplines is estimated to have boosted U.S. exports by $1 billion a year.[41]

Some critics argue that the OECD Arrangement is ineffective in disciplining the activities of OECD members that are not compliant with the agreement. For example, there is an OECD aircraft understanding that developed-country ECAs will not support export financing in other developed countries. However, a number of countries, such as Canada and Japan, may be doing so now. The Ex-Im Bank abides by this rule, but businesses are concerned that this practice places them at a competitive disadvantage. There are also questions about the relevance of the OECD Arrangement in light of the growing official export credit activity of non-OECD members such as China, Brazil, and India, who are not obligated to comply with the OECD limitations on the terms and conditions of export credit activity.

POTENTIAL OPTIONS FOR CONGRESS

A range of potential options are available to the 112th Congress as it considers reauthorization of the Ex-Im Bank. Some stakeholders may support or oppose the Bank generally, while others may be broadly supportive of the Bank but take issue with some of its specific policies and programs.

Structure of the Ex-Im Bank

Congress may examine the organizational structure of the Ex-Im Bank. Policy options include maintaining the Ex-Im Bank as an independent agency, reorganizing or privatizing the functions of the Bank, or terminating the Bank.

Maintain Status Quo
Congress could choose to maintain the status quo, keeping the Ex-Im Bank as an independent federal government agency that serves as the official ECA of the United States. Supporters of this option may argue that it would provide the Bank continuity in its current activities, maintain the Bank's current role in the federal government's export promotion efforts, allow the

Bank's transactions the benefits of being backed by the full faith and credit of the U.S. government, and avoid potential drawbacks of alternative policy options (described below). Critics may contend that maintaining the status quo neglects to address issues such as the effectiveness, efficiency, and relevance of the Bank in promoting exports through its credit and insurance programs.

Reorganize the Functions of the Bank

In recent years, there has been increased focus on possible reorganization of the U.S. government agencies involved in export promotion. On January 13, 2012, President Obama asked Congress for authority to reorganize and consolidate the business- and trade-related functions of six federal entities into one department in an effort to streamline the federal government. In addition to the Ex-Im Bank, the agencies included in the proposal were the Department of Commerce, Overseas Private Investment Corporation (OPIC), Small Business Administration (SBA), Trade and Development Agency (TDA), and the Office of the United States Trade Representative (USTR).[42]

Congress could conduct oversight, engage in consultations with the Administration, hold hearings, grant reorganizational authority to the President, work with the President on his proposal, and/or introduce and enact trade reorganization legislation separate from the President's plan. In terms of reorganization, there are a number of different approaches Congress could take. For example, Congress could consolidate all federal government trade functions—such as providing information, counseling, and export assistance services; funding feasibility studies; financing and insuring U.S. trade; conducting government-to-government advocacy; and negotiating new trade agreements and enforcing existing ones—into a new "Department of Trade." Alternatively, Congress could transfer all of the export financing functions of the Ex-Im Bank, USDA, and SBA into one centralized U.S. export credit agency.

Proponents of trade reorganization argue that consolidation may increase the effectiveness of federal export promotion efforts and reduce government costs, among other objectives. Supporters maintain that consolidation would also provide a more streamlined rationale for U.S. export promotion services based on more clearly defined goals. Critics contend that such proposals could result in the creation of a large federal bureaucracy, with little effect on the ability of the U.S. government to expand exports. Some stakeholders are concerned that consolidation of trade functions may result in federal export assistance that is not responsive to the specific needs of certain exporters, such as small- and medium-sized businesses or agricultural businesses. Terminating certain agencies may result in cost savings, but there may also be costs associated with transferring their functions, if deemed necessary, to other agencies.

Privatize the Functions of the Bank

Congress may consider privatizing the functions of the Ex-Im Bank. Central premises behind this option may include the fact that the Bank is self-sustaining, which is seen as proof that there is no market failure; concerns that the Bank may compete with or crowd out private sector export financing activity; and the notion that the private sector is more efficient and better suited than the federal government to conduct export financing activity. Such a proposal may also be rationalized by the view that it would shift the potential costs and risks of exporting away from the public sector, including U.S. taxpayers, and toward the private sector.

Others may oppose this option on the grounds that the federal government plays a unique role in its capacity to address market failures, which dampen the level of U.S. exports. Critics of privatizing Ex-Im Bank functions assert that the Bank's credit and insurance activities backed by the full faith and credit of the U.S. government may make certain export transactions, such as those for major infrastructure projects, more commercially attractive or may give the Bank leverage to guarantee repayment in a way that is not available to the private sector. In addition, critics of privatization may also contend that federal financing of exports is critical in times of financial crisis, which can lead to a shortfall in the private sector financing, and because of growing official export credit support by other countries. Furthermore, privatizing the Bank may raise logistical issues, such as how would the newly privatized entity issue securities and what would happen to existing export credit and insurance support obligations.

Terminate the Bank's Authority

Congress may consider terminating the Ex-Im Bank on the basis of a number of concerns, including the size and scope of the federal government, the economic rationale of the Bank, corporate welfare arguments, the impact of the Bank on taxpayers (because Ex-Im Bank financing is backed by the full faith and credit of the U.S. government), and the effectiveness of the Bank in promoting exports. The Ex-Im Bank receives significant support from the business community that is largely rooted in the belief that Ex-Im Bank programs equip U.S. firms with tools to compete with foreign firms that have access to similar support through their countries' ECAs. Business stakeholders generally contend that there are aspects of the Ex-Im Bank's programs and policies that could be improved to enhance the Bank's support for exports and would likely strongly oppose proposals to terminate the Bank. Thus, terminating the Bank may raise questions about the extent to which implementing the National Export Initiative could be successful without federal government export financing through the Ex-Im Bank.

Length of Reauthorization

If Congress chooses to reauthorize the Ex-Im Bank, it may debate the length of time to extend the Bank's authority. In recent years, Congress has extended the Ex-Im Bank's authority for a few years at a time. For example, the Export-Import Bank Reauthorization Act of 2002 (P.L. 107- 189) extended the Ex-Im Bank's authority for four years through FY2006, and the Export-Import Bank Reauthorization Act of 2006 (P.L. 109-438) extended the Ex-Im Bank's authority for five years through FY2011. Policy options related to reauthorization time length include

- maintaining status quo, extending the Ex-Im Bank's authority for a few years at a time;
- extending the Bank's authority for a longer period of time; or
- providing the Bank with a "permanent" reauthorization.

In considering the length of the reauthorization terms, some policymakers may argue that frequent reauthorizations allow for more opportunity for congressional oversight of Ex-Im Bank activities, while others may argue that longer-term or permanent reauthorizations would benefit the Ex-Im Bank's long-term strategic planning. To date, Ex-Im Bank's authority has never lapsed. If the Bank's authority were to lapse, it would not have the ability to approve any new authorizations of loans, guarantees, or insurance, but could continue to fulfill existing obligations.[43]

The Ex-Im Bank's Policies

Legislation to reauthorize the Ex-Im Bank has generally included not only extensions of the ExIm Bank's authority but, in some cases, congressional directives related to Ex-Im Bank programs and policies. Congress may examine the Ex-Im Bank's policies and consider some policy options.

Maintain Status Quo

Congress may choose to pass a "clean reauthorization" of the Ex-Im Bank that does not introduce any major changes to the Bank's policies. Some may argue that the Bank has proven to be an effective facilitator of U.S. exports and jobs in its nearly 70-year history and has demonstrated the important role that it plays in supporting exports during the international financial crisis. Proponents of this policy option may argue that Congress has struck a fair balance among the various stakeholder interests—such as business and labor interests—in its present requirements of the Ex-Im Bank and that adjustments to this balance are unwarranted. However, there have been a number of long-standing issues concerning the Bank raised by various stakeholder groups during previous congressional reauthorization debates that may continue to demand attention.

Revise the Ex-Im Bank's Policies

Congress could revise the Bank's policies related to the requirements and limitations on the ExIm Bank's credit and insurance activities. Congress could consider, as part of legislation to reauthorize the Bank, potential changes to some of the Ex-Im Bank's policies that stakeholders believe are detracting from the Ex-Im Bank's core mission of boosting U.S. exports and jobs. Congress could also consider revising the Bank's policies that relate to other policy interests, including supporting U.S. labor interests, protecting the environment, and promoting U.S. foreign policy and development objectives.

- Congress could examine and revise the Bank's policies related to domestic and foreign content, cargo preference requirements, the economic and environmental impact assessments, the tied aid war chest, and congressional mandates directing the Ex-Im Bank to target its support to specific types of exports. For example, Congress could direct the Bank to broaden what constitutes "national content" or direct the Bank to transform the economic and environmental considerations into "positive" requirements—that is, the Bank could support projects that benefit the domestic industry and employment and the environment, rather than be required to deny applications for financing for export contracts that have adverse effects.

- Congress could examine and revise other limitations on the Bank, such as the ceiling on the Ex-Im Bank's total credit and insurance exposure or the threshold amount at which the Bank is required to notify Congress about a proposed transaction before the Board of Directors grant final approval for the transaction.

In addressing such policy changes, Congress may attempt to strike a balance between export promotion and other public policy goals that might be in tension with export promotion. Congress also may seek to balance its interest in targeting Ex-Im Bank support for specific types of exports against the Bank's desire for flexibility in fulfilling its general mandate to support U.S. exports.

Global Competitiveness Issues

The increasingly competitive nature of international ECA activity raises new challenges for the Ex-Im Bank, both in terms of the international disciplines guiding ECA activity and the Ex-Im Bank's understanding of international export credit activity and trends. These challenges give rise to additional potential options for Congress.

Strengthen International Disciplines Guiding Official Export Credit Activity

Congress could examine and seek to strengthen the international disciplines guiding ECA activity, working to "update" these disciplines to reflect current trends in ECA activity by both developed and developing countries. For example, Congress could direct the United States to

- encourage greater engagement by the OECD with non-OECD emerging market economies, such as Brazil, China, and India, on official export credit activity;
- negotiate rules in the OECD that limit ECA financing in other developed countries; and
- pursue a greater role for the WTO in disciplining international ECA activity.

Supporters argue that such directives may help to level the playing field for U.S. exporters by reducing trade-distorting export credit competition and associated economic losses. Skeptics might argue that changes, if achieved, may be slow to materialize given the complex nature of multilateral and plurilateral negotiations. They could also argue that it may be difficult to include comprehensive rules on publicly backed export credit activity that cover both developed and developing countries.

Enhance Analysis and Understanding of Global Competitiveness Context
Congress may wish to explore how best to enhance the United States's understanding of the global competitiveness context in which the Bank and U.S. exporters operate. One possible avenue of focus would be to revise the Ex-Im Bank's annual competitiveness report, which is required by Congress and discusses the competitiveness of the Bank's financing services.[44] Congress could direct changes to the competiveness report, such as to enhance the comparative analysis, for example, to include more comprehensive data on the Ex-Im Bank's performance vis-à-vis other ECAs on the basis of volumes of transactions, types of products, industry sectors, and exporters supported.[45]

The introduction of additional requirements may allow more informed, updated analysis of the Ex-Im Bank's competitive position vis-à-vis foreign ECAs. Skeptics could argue that it may be difficult to access some of the additional comparative data about foreign ECAs. They could also argue that such requirements may pose increased demands on Ex-Im Bank resources.

LEGISLATIVE ACTION IN THE 112TH CONGRESS

Reauthorization of the Ex-Im Bank historically has been a fairly routine process in Congress. However, it became a more controversial debate in the 112th Congress, with the often divergent interests of various Members and stakeholders coming to the forefront—including business groups that support the Ex-Im Bank, seek a longer-term increase in the Bank's authority and a higher exposure cap, and contend that the Bank's support is critical in offsetting official international export credit competition; companies, including a U.S. airline company, that contend that the Bank's activities place them at a commercial disadvantage by benefiting foreign competitors; and other critics that consider the Bank to be a form of corporate welfare and question the role of government in export promotion and financing.[46]

The 112th Congress considered several pieces of legislation related to the Ex-Im Bank's reauthorization, ultimately passing an amended version of H.R. 2072 (Miller), the Export-Import Bank Reauthorization Act of 2012. As passed, H.R. 2072 extends the Ex-Im Bank's authority through FY2014. The bill includes other provisions, including to:

- increase the Bank's lending authority to $120 billion in FY2012, $130 billion in FY2013, and $140 billion in FY2014—with the increase in lending authority for FY2013 and FY2014 contingent on the Bank maintaining a "default rate" of less than 2% and on submitting various reports;

- require the Bank to monitor and report to Congress on the "default rate" of its financing, and, in the event that the rate exceeds 2%, to submit a report to Congress on a plan to reduce it to less than 2%;

- require the Bank to provide a notice and comment period for Bank transactions exceeding $100 million;

- require the Secretary of the Treasury to initiate and pursue negotiations with other major exporting countries, including members of the OECD and non-OECD members, to substantially reduce—with the ultimate goal of eliminating—subsidized export financing and other forms of export subsidies; to negotiate with all countries to eliminate all aircraft export credit financing by state-sponsored entities covered by the OECD Aircraft Sector Understanding; and to provide annual reports to Congress on the progress of such negotiations;

- require the Bank to develop and make publicly available methodological guidelines to be used by the Bank in conducting economic impact analyses of its transactions;

- require the Bank to review its national content policy, taking into consideration factors such as whether the policy captures both the direct and indirect costs of U.S. production of goods and services, the competitiveness of Ex-Im Bank's national content policy relative to foreign ECAs, the impact on the U.S. manufacturing and services workforce, any recommendations of the Ex-Im Bank Advisory Committee, and the impact of the policy on incentives to create or maintain operations in the United States and to increase the level of U.S. jobs;

- direct the Government Accountability Office (GAO) to analyze the Ex-Im Bank's methodology for calculating how many U.S. jobs are created or maintained through Ex-Im Bank support;

- prohibit Ex-Im Bank from supporting transactions with persons unless they self-certify that they are not engaged in sanctionable activities with respect to Iran, related to the Iran Sanctions Act of 1996; the Comprehensive Iran Sanctions, Accountability, and Divestment Act of 2010; and part 560 of Title 31 of the Code of Federal Regulations (commonly referred to as the "Iran Transactions Regulations"); require certification in the event that a person has engaged in sanctionable activity with respect to Iran, such that Ex-Im Bank financing would be prohibited unless the President has waived the imposition of sanctions on the person (such as for national interests reasons), pursuant to the Iran Sanctions Act of 1996 (P.L. 104-172), or has taken other specified actions;

- allow up to 1.25% of the surplus of the Bank during FY2012, FY2013, and FY2014 to be used to update the Bank's information technology systems;
- increase textile industry representation on the Ex-Im Bank's Advisory Committee;
- extend the Sub-Saharan Africa Advisory Committee until September 30, 2014; and
- increase other reporting requirements of the Bank, including provisions related to the Bank's exposure limit, risk management, and support for small business.

H.R. 2072 was introduced and referred to the House Financial Services Committee on June 1, 2011. The final version of H.R. 2072 passed by Congress reflects amendments to the bill adopted by the House, following a bipartisan compromise reached by the House majority leader and the House minority whip on May 4, 2012.

For example, as originally drafted, H.R. 2072 would have extended the Bank's authority for an additional year (to FY2015), would have incrementally increased the Bank's exposure cap to a higher level (to $160 billion in FY2014 and subsequent years), and did not include any requirements to conduct international negotiations to reduce and eliminate officially backed export credit financing.

On May 9, the House passed an amended version of H.R. 2072, considering the bill under suspension of the rules. The House passed the bill by a vote of 330-93.

On May 15, 2012, the Senate passed H.R. 2072, without further amendment by a vote of 78-20. Prior to voting on H.R. 2072, the Senate voted down five amendments concerning Ex-Im Bank activities in various ways:

- S.Amdt. 2100 (Lee) would have phased out the Ex-Im Bank's authority and required the President to initiate negotiations with other major exporting countries to end subsidized export financing.
- S.Amdt. 2101 (Paul) would have prohibited Ex-Im Bank financing for projects in a country in which the government or central bank holds debt instruments of the United States.
- S.Amdt. 2102 (Corker) would have included certification requirements for the Bank, such that the Bank could finance transactions only if foreign ECAs were providing financing for similar transactions, or in cases in which private sector financing was unavailable or prohibitively expensive. In addition, it would have required the Bank to maintain a ratio of capital to the outstanding principal balance of loans and loan guarantees of not less than 10%.
- S.Amdt. 2103 (Vitter), among other things, would have prohibited the Bank from making or guaranteeing a loan that is subordinate to any other loan; restricted financing of certain fossil fuel projects in foreign countries, related to cases in which the Ex-Im Bank identifies domestic fossil fuel projects that could benefit from Ex-Im Bank financing; and prohibited the extension of Ex-Im Bank credit for projects that involved the manufacture of renewable energy projects in foreign countries.
- S.Amdt. 2104 (Toomey) would have prohibited an increase in the Ex-Im Bank's lending authority to more than $100 billion until the Secretary of the Treasury certified that the Secretary had initiated international negotiations to eliminate export financing programs. It also would have prohibited an increase in the lending authority to $120 billion until a multilateral agreement to eliminate export financing has been completed.

In the Senate, the primary legislative vehicle for Ex-Im Bank reauthorization was S. 1547 (Johnson), the Export-Import Bank Reauthorization Act of 2011, which was introduced on September 13, 2011. It was reported by the Senate Banking, Housing, and Urban Affairs Committee and placed on the Senate Legislative Calendar under General Orders. Among other things, S. 1547 would have extended the Ex-Im Bank's authority through FY2015 and would have increased the Bank's lending authority incrementally to $110 billion in FY2012, $120 billion in FY2013, $130 billion in FY2014, and $140 billion in FY2015. The final version of H.R. 2072 reflects certain provisions from the Senate legislation, including enhanced transparency and accountability requirements for the Bank, stronger restrictions against companies doing business with Iran, and revised domestic content requirements. [47]

Prior to final consideration of H.R. 2072, several other pieces of legislation were considered that also would have extended the Ex-Im Bank's authority. For example, S.Amdt. 1836 (Cantwell) was offered as an amendment to the Jumpstart Our Business Startups Act (H.R. 3606, P.L. 112 106). Like S. 1547, the amendment would have extended the Bank's authority through FY2015 and would have increased its exposure cap incrementally to $140 billion in FY2015. A cloture motion on the amendment did not pass, and it was ruled non-germane. The amendment subsequently was introduced in the House as H.R. 4302 (Larsen). Legislation also was introduced in the Congress to terminate the Ex-Im Bank (H.R. 4268, Amash).

End Notes

[1] For a general background on Ex-Im Bank, see CRS Report R42472, *Export-Import Bank: Background and Legislative Issues*, by Shayerah Ilias. For a general background on federal export promotion agencies, see CRS Report R41495, *U.S. Government Agencies Involved in Export Promotion: Overview and Issues for Congress*, coordinated by Shayerah Ilias.

[2] *Report to the President on the National Export Initiative: The Export Promotion Cabinet's Plan for Doubling U.S. Exports in Five Years*, Washington, DC, September 2010, http://www.whitehouse.gov/sites/default/files/nei_report_9- 16-10_full.pdf.

[3] Ex-Im Bank, Lender Referral List, updated November 2010, http://www.exim.gov/pub/pdf/ebd-g-01.pdf. Ex-Im Bank, Active Insurance Brokers Registered with Ex-Im Bank, http://www.exim.gov/news/brokers_list.cfm. Ex-Im Bank, Working Capital Guarantee Delegated Authority Lenders, updated November 30, 2011, http://www.exim.gov/pub/pdf/ebd-w-13.pdf.

[4] Ex-Im Bank, *City/State Partners List*, last updated March 29, 2011, http://www.exim.gov/about/partners/citystate/ citystate_partnerslist_updated.cfm.

[5] U.S. Congress, House Committee on Financial Services, Subcommittee on International Monetary Policy and Trade, *Statement for the Record from the Coalition for Employment through Exports*, 112th Cong., 1st sess., March 10, 2011.

[6] The G-7 consists of Canada, France, Germany, Italy, Japan, the United Kingdom, and the United States. Data from Ex-Im Bank, *Report to the U.S. Congress on Export Credit Competition and the Export-Import Bank of the United States, For the Period January 1, 2010 through December 31, 2010*, Washington, DC, June 2011, p. 5.

[7] For more information on the various international disciplines, see http://www.oecd.org/department/ 0,3355,en_2649_34171_1_1_1_1_1,00.html for the OECD, http://www.berneunion.org.uk/ for the Berne Union, and http://www.wto.org /english/tratop_e/scm_e/scm_e.htm for the WTO.

[8] See footnote 5 to SCM Article 3.1(a) and paragraph (k) of the Illustrative List of Export Subsidies, Annex I to the SCM Agreement. Paragraph (k) states: "Provided, however, that if

a Member is a party to an international undertaking on official export credits to which at least twelve original Members to this Agreement are parties as of 1 January 1979 (or a successor undertaking which has been adopted by those original Members), or if in practice a Member applies the interest rates provisions of the relevant undertaking, an export credit practice which is in conformity with those provisions shall not be considered an export subsidy prohibited by this Agreement."

[9] Berne Union, *Guiding Principles*, http://www.berneunion.org.uk/guiding-principles.html.

[10] Paul Brewer, "Australia's Export Promotion Program: Is it Effective?," *Australian Journal of Management*, vol. 34, no. 1 (June 2009), pp. 125-142.

[11] Brazil, while not party to the OECD Arrangement, is party to the OECD Aircraft Sector Understanding.

[12] For instance, The Boeing Company, a significant beneficiary of Ex-Im Bank services, notes that the European aircraft manufacturer Airbus, its main competitor in the aerospace sector, has three European ECAs supporting its sales. Boeing further states, the competitive landscape for our industry is about to get a lot more crowded. Companies in Canada, Russia, Brazil, and China are developing large commercial airplanes to compete with Boeing, and all of them have government export credit agencies to support them. In today's competitive global market, financing often is a key discriminator, and foreign governments are offering export credit to the advantage of their domestic industries. U.S. Congress, House Committee on Financial Services, Subcommittee on International Monetary Policy and Trade, Testimony of Scott Scherer, Boeing Capital Corporation, on the Role of the U.S. Export-Import Bank in Ensuring U.S. Competitiveness and Job Creation, 112th Cong., 1st sess., March 10, 2011.

[13] U.S. Congress, House Committee on Financial Services, Subcommittee on International Monetary Policy and Trade, *Statement for the Record from the Coalition for Employment through Exports*, 112th Cong., 1st sess., March 10, 2011.

[14] Ex-Im Bank, *Report to the U.S. Congress on Export Credit Competition and the Export-Import Bank of the United States, For the Period January 1, 2010 through December 31, 2010*, Washington, DC, June 2011, p. 13.

[15] U.S. Congress, House Committee on Financial Services, Subcommittee on International Monetary Policy and Trade, *Statement for the Record from the Coalition for Employment through Exports*, 112th Cong., 1st sess., March 10, 2011.

[16] Ex-Im Bank, *Report to the U.S. Congress on Export Credit Competition and the Export-Import Bank of the United States, For the Period January 1, 2009 through December 31, 2009*, Washington, DC, June 2010, p. 99.

[17] Meeting with Ex-Im Bank officials, May 5, 2011.

[18] Berne Union, press release, July 12, 2010, http://www.berneunion.org.uk/pdf/Press%20Release%20July%202010.pdf.

[19] U.S. Government Accountability Office, *U.S. Export-Import Bank: Actions Needed to Promote Competitiveness and International Cooperation*, GAO-12-294, February 2012.

[20] Coalition for Employment through Exports (CEE), *2011 Supplier Study*.

[21] 12 U.S.C §635e.

[22] Rossella Brevetti, "CEE Urges Congress to Pass Ex-Im Reauthorization This Year," *International Trade Daily*, December 13, 2011.

[23] U.S. Congress, Senate Committee on Banking, Housing, and Urban Affairs, *Oversight and Reauthorization of the Export-Import Bank of the United States*, Testimony of Fred P. Hochberg - President and Chairman, Export-Import Bank of the United States, 112th Cong., 1st sess., May 17, 2011.

[24] Ibid., pp. 26, 37.

[25] See Ex-Im Bank's content policies for more details: http://www.exim.gov/products /policies/foreign_mediumlong.cfm.

[26] Ex-Im Bank, *Report to the U.S. Congress on Export Credit Competition and the Export-Import Bank of the United States, For the Period January 1, 2010 through December 31, 2011*, Washington, DC, June 2011, p. 81.

[27] Coalition for Employment through Exports (CEE), "Ex-Im Bank 2011 Reauthorization: CEE Position Paper."

[28] U.S. Congress, House Committee on Financial Services, Subcommittee on International Monetary Policy and Trade, *Statement of Karan Bhatia, Vice President & Senior Counsel, International Law & Policy, General Electric*, 112th Cong., 1st sess., March 10, 2011.

[29] Ex-Im Bank, *Report to the U.S. Congress on Export Credit Competition and the Export-Import Bank of the United States, For the Period January 1, 2010 through December 31, 2010*, Washington, DC, June 2011, p. 57.

[30] U.S. Congress, House Committee on Financial Services, Subcommittee on International Monetary Policy and Trade, *Statement for the Record from the Coalition for Employment through Exports*, 112th Cong., 1st sess., March 10, 2011.

[31] *Report to the President on the National Export Initiative: The Export Promotion Cabinet's Plan for Doubling U.S. Exports in Five Years*, Washington, DC, September 2010, http://www.whitehouse.gov/sites/default/files/nei_report_9-16-10_full.pdf.

[32] Ex-Im Bank, *Report to the U.S. Congress on Export Credit Competition and the Export-Import Bank of the United States, For the Period January 1, 2010 through December 31, 2010*, Washington, DC, June 2011, p. 42.

[33] Ex-Im Bank, *Ex-Im Bank Policies: Shipping Requirements (MARAD)*, http://www.exim.gov/products/policies/ shipping.cfm. Maritime Administration, *U.S.-Flag Waterborne Domestic Trade and Related Programs*, http://www.marad.dot.gov /ships_shipping_landing_page/domestic_shipping/Domestic_Shipping.htm.

[34] U.S. Congress, House Committee on Financial Services, Subcommittee on International Monetary Policy and Trade, *Statement of USA Maritime*, Hearing on the Role of the Export-Import Bank in U.S. Competitiveness and Job Creation, 112th Cong., 1st sess., March 11, 2011.

[35] Ibid.

[36] Coalition for Employment through Exports, *Ex-Im Bank 2011 Reauthorization: CEE Position Paper*.

[37] U.S. Congress, House Committee on Financial Services, Subcommittee on International Monetary Policy and Trade, *Statement for the Record from the Coalition for Employment through Exports*, 112th Cong., 1st sess., March 10, 2011.

[38] "Airlines Press Ahead With Ex-Im Bank Lawsuit After Judge Denies Injunction," *Inside U.S. Trade's World Trade Online*, February 9, 2012. Josh Mitchell and Corey Boles, "Boeing, Delta Class on Exports," *The Wall Street Journal*, March 16, 2012.

[39] Ex-Im Bank, *Report to the U.S. Congress on Export Credit Competition and the Export-Import Bank of the United States, For the Period January 1, 2010 through December 31, 2010*, Washington, DC, June 2011, p. 67.

[40] U.S. Congress, House Committee on Financial Services, *Ex-Im Bank Oversight: The Role of Trade Finance in Doubling Exports over Five Years*, Fred P. Hochberg, President and Chairman of the Export-Import Bank, 111th Cong., September 29, 2010.

[41] Office of the U.S. Trade Representative, *The Organization for Economic Cooperation and Development (OECD)*, http://www.ustr.gov/trade-agreements/wto-multilateral-affairs/oecd.

[42] The White House, "Government Reorganization Fact Sheet," press release, January 13, 2012, http://www.whitehouse.gov/the-press-office/2012/01/13/government-reorganization-fact-sheet. For additional information on the reorganization process, see CRS Report R41841, *Executive Branch Reorganization Initiatives During the 112th Congress: A Brief Overview*, by Henry B. Hogue.

[43] The restrictions on Ex-Im Bank's activities in the event of an authorization lapse are set forth in Section 7 of the Export-Import Bank of 1945, as amended (codified at 12 U.S.C. §635f).

[44] 12 U.S.C. §635 g-1. The Ex-Im Bank's Charter requires that the competitiveness report discusses actions by the Bank in providing financing on a competitive basis, and to minimize government-supported export financing; the role of the Bank in implementing the strategic plan prepared by the Trade Promotion Coordinating Committee; the Bank's tied aid credit program and fund; the purpose of Bank transactions (such as to address market failure, matching support); the efforts of the Bank to promote exports of goods and services related to renewable energy sources; the size of the Bank account; co-financing programs of the Bank and other foreign ECAs; services supported by the Bank and other ECAs; export finance cases not in compliance with the OECD Arrangement; and foreign ECA activities not consistent with the WTO SCM Agreement.

[45] Ex-Im Bank, *Report to the U.S. Congress on Export Credit Competition and the Export-Import Bank of the United States*, For the Period January 1, 2009 through December 31, 2009, Washington, DC, June 2010, p. 1.

[46] Joseph J. Schatz, "Cantor, Hoyer Reach Ex-Im Bank Authorization Deal," *Congressional Quarterly Today*, May 7, 2012.

[47] "Johnson Applauds Passage of Export-Import Bank Reauthorization," press release, May 15, 2012, http://banking.senate.gov/public/index.cfm?FuseAction=Newsroom.Press Releases& ContentRecord_id=55ecb57bd9f7-2509-e259-00b0d5f33f0a.

In: The Export-Import Bank of the United States   ISBN: 978-1-62618-709-2
Editor: Fraser M. Mulder   © 2013 Nova Science Publishers, Inc.

Chapter 3

U.S. EXPORT-IMPORT BANK: ACTIONS NEEDED TO PROMOTE COMPETITIVENESS AND INTERNATIONAL COOPERATION[*]

United States Government Accountability Office

WHY GAO DID THIS STUDY

The U.S. Export-Import Bank (Ex-Im), the United States' official export credit agency (ECA), helps U.S. firms export goods and services by providing a range of financial products. Ex-Im, whose primary mission is to support jobs through exports, has a range of policy requirements, including support of small business. The Organisation for Economic Cooperation and Development (OECD) Arrangement governs aspects of U.S. and some foreign countries' ECAs. GAO examined (1) Ex-Im's mission and organization compared with ECAs from other Group of Seven (G-7) countries (major industrialized countries that consult on economic issues), (2) ExIm's policy requirements compared with other G-7 ECAs, (3) Ex-Im's domestic content policy compared with other G-7 ECAs, and (4) the OECD Arrangement's role in governing ECA activities.

---

[*] This is an edited, reformatted and augmented version of United States Government Accountability Office, Publication No. GAO-12-294, dated February 2012.

WHAT GAO RECOMMENDS

GAO recommends (1) that Ex-Im conduct a systematic review to assess how well its domestic content policy continues to support Ex-Im's mission, and (2) that the Department of the Treasury, with Ex-Im and international counterparts, develop strategies for further engagement on export credit issues with emerging economy countries. Ex-Im stated it considers content policy in its annual competitiveness assessments, but did not comment directly on the recommendation. Treasury stated it supports encouraging emerging market economies' participation concerning export credit issues and is engaged in that activity, but did not state whether it agreed with the recommendation.

WHAT GAO FOUND

The United States and other G-7 countries have ECAs that support domestic exports, but Ex-Im differs from other ECAs in several important ways, including its explicit mission to promote domestic employment. The G-7 ECAs range from government agencies to private companies contracted by governments. Most of these ECAs, including Ex-Im, are expected to supplement, not compete with, the private market. Ex-Im offers direct loans, which were increasingly utilized during the recent financial crisis, while European ECAs do not.

Ex-Im has specific mandates in areas where other G-7 ECAs have broad directives. Ex-Im has specific mandates to support small business and environmentally beneficial exports, while other ECAs are broadly directed to support such exports. In addition, Ex-Im has other mandates and legal requirements, such as shipping certain exports on U.S.-flagged carriers and conducting economic impact assessments for large transactions, which other G-7 ECAs do not.

Ex-Im's requirements for the level of domestic content in the exports it fully finances are higher and generally less flexible than those of other G-7 ECAs. ExIm requires 85 percent domestic content for medium- and long-term transactions to receive full financing, while other ECAs' domestic content requirements generally range between zero and 51 percent. Ex-Im's policy on supporting local costs can result in more foreign content support in some transactions. While ExIm has modified its method for calculating domestic content, its threshold for receiving full financing for medium- and long-term transactions has not changed since 1987, and the policy and its overall impact on jobs has not been studied systematically. Other ECAs have modified their policies in recent years, citing increasing global content of industrial production. In its charter, Ex-Im is directed to provide financing competitive with that of other ECAs, as well as to support U.S. jobs.

The OECD Arrangement has expanded to regulate additional aspects of officially supported export credits, but increasing activity of nonmembers threatens its ability to provide a level playing field for exporters. Several agreements have been made that decrease subsidies and increase transparency among ECAs. However, these agreements apply only to participant ECAs, and important emerging countries, including China, are not part of the Arrangement. Officials from several G-7 ECAs and other institutions identified effective engagement with these countries on export credit issues as being increasingly important and presenting challenges for the OECD Arrangement and its participants.

ABBREVIATIONS

CEO	chief executive officer
CIRR	Commercial Interest Reference Rate
Coface	Compagnie Française d'Assurance pour le Commerce Extérieur
CRS	Congressional Research Service
ECA	export credit agency
ECGD	Export Credits Guarantee Department
EDC	Export Development Canada
EU	European Union
G-7	Group of Seven
GDP	gross domestic product
JBIC	Japanese Bank for International Cooperation
KfW	KfW Bankengruppe
NEXI	Nippon Export and Investment Insurance
OECD	Organisation for Economic Cooperation and Development
OPIC	Overseas Private Investment Corporation
SACE	Servizi Assicurativi del Commercio Estero
SBA	Small Business Administration
SIMEST	Societa Italiana per le Imprese all'Estero
UK	United Kingdom

February 7, 2012
The Honorable Gary Miller
Chairman
International Monetary Policy
and Trade Subcommittee

The Honorable Judy Biggert
Chairman
Insurance, Housing and Community
Opportunity Subcommittee
Committee on Financial Services
House of Representatives

The Honorable Gregory Meeks
House of Representatives

As the nation's official export credit agency (ECA), the U.S. Export-Import Bank (Ex-Im) supports U.S. exporters by providing loans, guarantees, and insurance, particularly during times of economic crisis when private financing is not available. Ex-Im's primary mission is to create U.S. jobs through exports. In addition, Ex-Im has a variety of other policy requirements, including congressional mandates to support small businesses and promote environmentally beneficial exports, as well as policies regarding the amount of U.S. content in the exports it finances. In its charter, Ex-Im is directed to provide financing competitive with the rates, terms, and other conditions available from other ECAs.

An international agreement, the Organisation for Economic Cooperation and Development (OECD) Arrangement on Officially Supported Export Credits (the Arrangement), governs various aspects of U.S. and other member countries' ECAs.[1] The Arrangement aims to promote a level playing field where exporters compete on the basis of price and quality rather than export credit support, including any subsidies. The Group of Seven (G-7) major industrialized countries are all participants in the Arrangement. However, some countries with substantial export credit activity—including China, India, and Brazil—are not participants in this agreement.

In the context of Ex-Im's latest reauthorization, Congress asked GAO to examine how Ex-Im's export credit support and policy requirements compare with those of other export credit agencies in developed countries. This review examines (1) Ex-Im's mission, organization, market orientation, and product offerings compared with those of the other G-7 ECAs; (2) Ex-Im's policy requirements compared with those of the other G-7 ECAs; (3) Ex-Im's domestic content policy compared with those of the other G-7 ECAs; and (4) the role of the OECD Arrangement in governing ECA activities.

To address these objectives, we reviewed relevant documentation related to Ex-Im and the other G-7 ECAs, including legislation, annual reports, OECD and academic reports, and Ex-Im's annual Competitiveness Reports. We met with officials from the following ECAs: Export Development Canada (EDC) in Canada, Coface in France, Export Credits Guarantee Department (ECGD) in the United Kingdom, Servizi Assicurativi del Commercio Estero (SACE) in Italy, and Hermes in Germany. We also met with officials from oversight organizations in G-7 countries, as well as the OECD and the Berne Union, an association of export credit and investment insurance providers. We spoke via telephone with officials from the Japanese ECAs, the Japanese Bank for International Cooperation (JBIC) and Nippon Export and Investment Insurance (NEXI). We interviewed Ex-Im officials from various divisions of the organization. We also spoke with officials from other U.S. government agencies, including the Departments of the Treasury and State, as well as the Small Business Administration. We interviewed a variety of experts on China's export credit activities, including experts at American University and the Brookings Institution. Appendix I provides more information on our scope and methodology.

We conducted this performance audit from February 2011 to February 2012 in accordance with generally accepted government auditing standards. Those standards require that we plan and perform the audit to obtain sufficient, appropriate evidence to provide a reasonable basis for our findings and conclusions based on our audit objectives. We believe that the evidence obtained provides a reasonable basis for our findings and conclusions based on our audit objectives.

BACKGROUND

Export credits are financing arrangements designed to mitigate risks to buyers and sellers associated with international transactions.[2] Export credits generally take the form of direct loans, loan guarantees, and export credit insurance, and may be short-term (0-1 year), medium-term (1-7 years), and long-term (7 plus years).[3] (See textbox below.) Buyers and sellers in international transactions face unique risks, such as foreign exchange risk, difficulties in settling disputes when damages to shipments occur, or instability in the buyer's country. For these reasons, lenders may be reluctant to finance a buyer's purchase of foreign goods. Export credit products are meant to facilitate international transactions by mitigating these risks. Official ECAs are organizations that provide export credits with explicit government backing, where either the government, or the government-owned ECA, assumes the risk and is financially liable for reimbursing the exporter or the lending institution if the buyer fails to pay.

ECA Export Credit Products Defined

- Export credit insurance: An insurance policy that protects the exporter from the risk of nonpayment by foreign buyers for commercial and political reasons.
- Loan guarantee: An ECA guarantees a lender's financing to an international buyer of goods or services, promising to pay the lender if the buyer defaults.
- Direct loan: The ECA makes a fixed-rate loan directly to an international buyer of goods and services.
- Interest make-up: In lieu of making direct loans, an ECA pays a lender the difference between the OECD minimum interest rate and commercial interest rates.

Ex-Im, the official export credit agency of the United States, is an independent government agency operating under the Export-Import Bank Act of 1945, as amended. Ex-Im currently has about 400 employees. Its mission is to support U.S. exports and jobs by providing export financing on terms that are competitive with those of official export credit support offered by other governments. Since fiscal year 2008, Ex-Im has been "self-sustaining" for appropriations purposes, financing its operations from receipts collected from its borrowers.[4] Ex-Im provides export credit insurance, direct loans, and loan guarantees in support of U.S. exports. In fiscal year 2011, Ex-Im authorized $32.7 billion: $7.0 billion in export credit insurance, $6.3 billion in direct loans, and $19.4 billion in loan guarantees. Ex-Im has a risk exposure limit of $100 billion, meaning that the total outstanding value of all loans, guarantees, and insurance contracts cannot exceed this number; at the end of fiscal year 2011, ExIm had a total exposure of $89.2 billion.

The other G-7 countries, which include some of the largest exporters, all have at least one ECA. See figure 1.

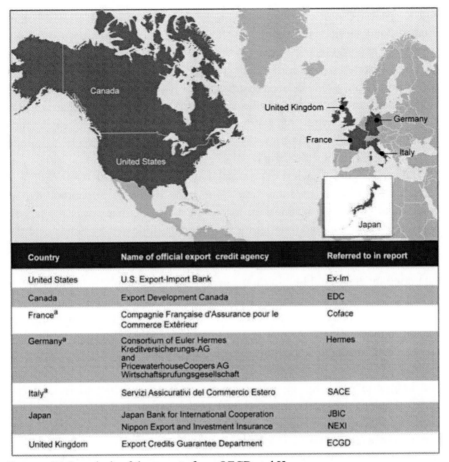

Country	Name of official export credit agency	Referred to in report
United States	U.S. Export-Import Bank	Ex-Im
Canada	Export Development Canada	EDC
France[a]	Compagnie Française d'Assurance pour le Commerce Extérieur	Coface
Germany[a]	Consortium of Euler Hermes Kreditversicherungs-AG and PricewaterhouseCoopers AG Wirtschaftsprufungsgesellschaft	Hermes
Italy[a]	Servizi Assicurativi del Commercio Estero	SACE
Japan	Japan Bank for International Cooperation	JBIC
	Nippon Export and Investment Insurance	NEXI
United Kingdom	Export Credits Guarantee Department	ECGD

Source: GAO analysis of documents from OECD and Hermes.

[a]France, Italy, and Germany each have an additional government or government-directed institution that offers products that could be characterized as officially supported export credits. Societa Italiana per le Imprese all'Estero (SIMEST) in Italy and Natixis in France have interest make-up programs. KfW IPEX-Bank in Germany offers loans at the OECD minimum interest rate in support of export-related transactions.

Figure 1. Official Export Credit Agencies of the G-7 Countries.

G-7 ECAs differ in the magnitude and types of their activities. All offer medium- and long-term officially supported export credits. According to Ex-Im, this financing is subject to the most intense international competition, where the support of an ECA can influence who wins overseas deals. Ex-Im's annual competitiveness reports compare ECAs on the basis of their medium-

and long-term export credit support programs. ECAs also can provide other products and services in addition to these medium- and long-term officially supported export credits; some of the G-7 ECAs offer short-term export credits, market-based export credits (called "market windows"), and other non-export credit products such as investment insurance. This can complicate comparisons among institutions, as some ECAs offer products that are also offered by other types of institutions, such as development or finance institutions, in other countries. ECAs do not typically compete with one another in the area of short-term credits.

Figure 2 shows each ECA's total new business in 2010, providing a comparison between medium- and long-term officially supported export credits and other new business in that same year. Germany was the largest provider of medium- and long-term export credits, followed by France and the United States. Japan's two ECAs, combined, had the largest amount of total new business in 2010, but only a very small portion was for officially supported medium- and long-term export credits; the remainder included other products such as overseas investment loans, untied loans, and overseas untied loan insurance.[5] This was also true of Canada's ECA, EDC, which had the second highest volume of total new business. A large proportion of the new business was attributable to short-term credit insurance.

The G-7 ECAs have historically accounted for the majority of medium- and long-term officially supported export credits, according to Ex-Im. The share of national exports financed by official export credit agencies is not large; on average, medium- and long-term ECA financing as a share of total exports for each of the G-7 countries in 2008 was 0.6 percent. The United Kingdom's (UK) share was lowest at 0.1 percent, and Italy's was the highest at 1.2 percent; the remaining G-7 countries ranged between those values.[6] However, ECAs do play a large role in certain sectors, such as aircraft. According to Ex-Im, at its peak in 2009, ECA financing represented about 40 percent of the total worldwide market for aircraft financing. In addition, the recent financial crisis has increased the amount of ECA support for exports; most G-7 ECAs saw notable increases in the volume of their medium- and long-term officially supported export credits starting in 2008 or 2009 because private sector lenders and insurers were either unwilling or unable to support transactions on their own. See figure 3 for estimates of the volume of medium- and long-term officially supported export credits provided by each G-7 country over the past 5 years.[7]

U.S. dollars (in billions)

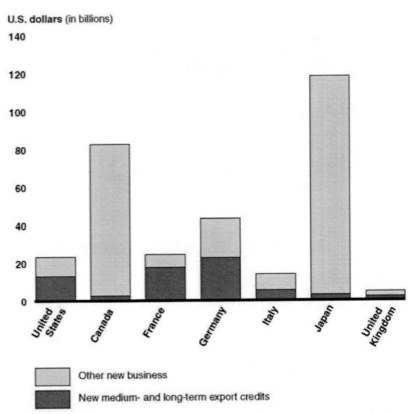

Source: Report to the U.S. Congress on Export Credit Competition and the Export-Import Bank of the United States, period January 2010-December 2010, and GAO analysis of ECA annual reports.

Notes: "Other new business" is calculated as the difference between "total new business" and new medium- and long-term export credits. "Total new business" is reported differently depending on the ECA. For the United States, data are for total authorizations. For Canada, it represents financial arrangements facilitated. For France, Germany, Italy, and the United Kingdom, it means new guarantees. For Japan, it is loan, guarantee, and investment commitments from JBIC, as well as the total underwritten amount from NEXI.

The "total new business" number for Japan is for fiscal year 2010 (April 2010-March 2011), while the number for medium- and long-term official export credits is an Ex-Im estimate for calendar year 2010. For the United Kingdom, the "total new business" number is for fiscal year 2010 (April 2010-March 2011), while the number for medium- and long-term official export credits is for calendar year 2010.

Figure 2. New Business by G-7 Export Credit Agency, 2010.

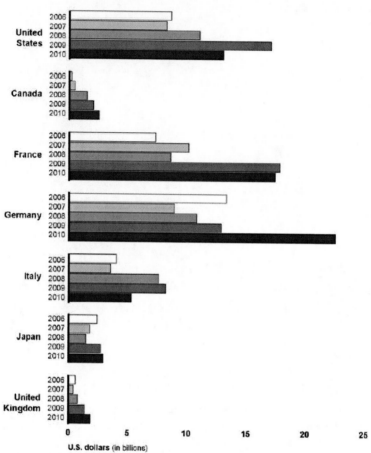

Note: Data represent the medium- and long-term officially supported export credits issued each year by country. U.S. data are presented on a calendar-year basis. Data for Canada exclude market window and domestic financing. For France, figures have been adjusted to exclude defense. Data for Italy exclude untied or domestic activity. Figures for Japan reflect an aggregation of JBIC export loans and an estimate of NEXI medium- and long-term official export cover; the 2010 figure for Japan is an Ex-Im estimate (data were not available).

Figure 3. Medium- and Long-Term Official Export Credits, 2006-2010.

The OECD Arrangement on Officially Supported Export Credits is a set of nonbinding rules among some OECD countries concluded in 1978 amid increases in ECAs' provision of officially supported export credits. The purpose of the Arrangement is to provide a framework for the use of officially supported export credits; to promote a level playing field, where competition is based on the price and quality of the exported goods and not the financial terms provided; and to provide transparency over programs and transactions. Participants to the Arrangement are Australia, Canada, the European Union (EU),[8] Japan, South Korea, New Zealand, Norway, Switzerland, and the United States. Other countries may join following invitation and OECD membership is not required. In addition, countries may belong to one or more of the Arrangement's sector agreements—for example, Brazil is a member of the Aircraft Sector Understanding—without being a full-fledged participant.

The Arrangement applies to officially supported export credits with repayment terms of 2 years or more. It places limitations on the terms and conditions, such as interest rates, length of repayment terms, and risk fees, of export credits that benefit from official support, and it also contains a variety of reporting requirements to ensure transparency. Another requirement is a down payment of 15 percent of an export contract's value. [9] The Arrangement and its various sector agreements are negotiated among participants and updated on an as-needed basis.[10]

In addition to the OECD Arrangement, another export credit committee at the OECD, the Working Party on Export Credits and Credit Guarantees (Export Credit Group), was set up in 1963. Its general objectives are to evaluate export credit policies, identify and resolve problems by multilateral discussion, work out common guiding principles, and improve cooperation between countries. To date, the Export Credit Group has been the venue for important export credit agreements on antibribery, environmental screening, and sustainable lending. All OECD countries except Chile and Iceland are members.

The U.S. Department of the Treasury's Office of Trade Finance has lead responsibility within the U.S. government for the development, implementation, and enforcement of international trade and aid finance policy, and its primary goal is to create and maintain a market-based, competitive environment in which governments' financing of national exports contains minimal subsidies.

The Office of Trade Finance leads the U.S. delegation to the OECD Arrangement. Other members of the delegation include Ex-Im, the Departments of Commerce and State, the Office of the U.S. Trade Representative, the U.S. Agency for International Development, the U.S. Trade and Development Agency, and other agencies whose programs or roles might be affected by the negotiations.

Ex-Im Differs from the Other G-7 ECAs in Several Important Ways, Including Its Explicit Mission to Promote Domestic Employment

Ex-Im is different from other G-7 ECAs in several significant ways, including its mission, which is explicitly focused on creating domestic jobs through exports. It is similar in its role as a lender/insurer of last resort to four other ECAs, while Canada and Italy have commercial market orientations and are not restricted from competing with the private market. As an independent government agency, Ex-Im's governance and organization type differ from those of other ECAs, which range from government departments to private companies contracted by governments. Ex-Im and other G-7 ECAs offer a different mix of export credit and other financing products, which provides them with different tools to help exporters. Ex-Im has an advantage over some of the other ECAs because it offers direct loans, which were useful during the financial crisis.

ECAs Differ in Their Missions and Organization Types

Ex-Im's mission strongly emphasizes supporting domestic jobs through exports, which is unique among the G-7 ECAs (see table 1). This aim underlies certain Ex-Im policies, such as its economic impact analysis requirement and its domestic content policy. Other ECA missions range from promoting and supporting domestic exports to securing natural resources.

Along with its mission is the ECA's "market orientation"—whether an export credit agency supplements or competes with private markets for export credit support. Most G-7 ECAs are directed to supplement the private market; that is, they play a role as a "lender or insurer of last resort," providing financing, guarantees, or insurance for transactions that are too risky or are undesirable for commercial support. In addition, according to G-7 ECA officials, European ECAs must abide by EU law prohibiting them from supporting short-term export credits to other EU member states and most OECD countries—transactions that the private market is willing to support. Ex-Im's role as a lender of last resort is emphasized in its charter. It must report the purpose for each transaction it supports, either to provide financing where private sector financing is unavailable or to meet foreign competition.

Table 1. Missions and Related Characteristics of the G-7 ECAs

Country: ECA	Stated mission	General market orientation	ECA organization type	ECA governance and decision-making authority
United States: Ex-Im	Supports U.S. domestic jobs through exports by providing export financing that is competitive with support offered by other governments	Lender /insurer of last resort	Independent government agency	Ex-Im has a board of directors appointed by the President and confirmed by the Senate. The board approves transactions above $10 million.[a]
Canada: EDC	Supports and develops Canada's domestic and export trade and Canadian capacity to respond to domestic and international business opportunities[b]	Commercial market orientation	Company wholly owned by the government (Canadian Crown Corporation)	A board of directors, appointed by the Minister for International Trade and composed of representatives primarily from the private sector, governs EDC and approves transactions.[c]
France: Coface	Promotes and supports French exports and foreign investments in the medium and long terms	Insurer of last resort	Private company contracted by the government	In addition to its private sector activities, Coface manages a separate account for state export credits and reports to the Ministry of Finance, which takes decisions on the largest and most important transactions.
Germany: Hermes	Promotes German exports; insures against the risk of nonpayment for commercial and political reasons; opens new markets, especially in emerging countries; and supports foreign customers, particularly those in difficult phases of development and restructuring	Insurer of last resort	Consortium of two private companies contracted by the government	The consortium manages export credits on behalf of the government, but an Interministerial Committee made up of the Ministries of Economics and Technology, Finance, Economic Cooperation and Development, and the Federal Foreign Office, make the approval decisions on transactions over 5 million euros.

Table 1. (Continued)

Country: ECA	Stated mission	General market orientation	ECA organization type	ECA governance and decision-making authority
Italy: SACE	Supports Italian exporters and the internationalization of Italian companies and banks	Commercial market orientation	Joint stock company with shares owned by the Ministry of Economy and Finance	A board of directors is appointed by the Ministry of Economy and Finance in agreement with the Ministry for Economic Development.
				Decisions on SACE's activity are made by the Board of Directors, which also provides the Chairman and the Chief Executive Officer (CEO) with specific powers of attorney.
Japan: JBIC and NEXI	JBIC: Secures natural resources, ensures competitiveness of Japanese companies, responds to disruptions in the international economy, and improves the environment; NEXI: Contributes to Japan's economy by anticipating changes in the market, responding to customer needs, and conducting insurance business in covering risks that arise in international transactions but are not covered by regular commercial insurance	JBIC: lender of last resort/ NEXI: somewhere between an insurer of last resort and commercial market orientation[d]	Companies whose shares are owned by the Ministry of Finance (JBIC) and the Ministry of Economy, Trade and Industry (NEXI)	JBIC: JBIC's parent institution, Japan Finance Corporation, has a governor who approves transactions over a certain threshold. JBIC's CEO or other executives approve all other transactions. NEXI: The Ministry of Economy, Trade and Industry approves transactions over a certain threshold. NEXI's Chairman or a Director approves all other transactions. The Board of Directors is an advisory body rather than a decision-making body.

Country: ECA	Stated mission	General market orientation	ECA organization type	ECA governance and decision-making authority
United Kingdom: ECGD	Complements the private market by providing assistance to exporters and investors, principally in the form of insurance and guarantees to banks	Insurer of last resort	Department of the government	An Executive Committee composed of ECGD Directors advises the Chief Executive on the management of ECGD's business. A subcommittee—Risk Committee—approves transactions.

Source: GAO analysis of ECA documents and interviews with ECA officials.

[a] According to Ex-Im, the threshold for board approval for medium- and long-term transactions is generally $10 million. However, there are exceptions to this general rule. For example, all nuclear-related transactions, irrespective of transaction value, must go to the board for approval after an intraagency clearance and congressional review process. For other products, such as short-term insurance and working capital guarantees, the approval threshold varies depending on the specific product.

[b] EDC's mandate was temporarily expanded to include a domestic component in 2009.

[c] The Chairperson of the board is appointed by the Governor in Council.

[d] NEXI officials said that while NEXI has a complementary relationship with the private sector, NEXI does not have a clear role as an insurer of last resort. Rather, NEXI sees itself as somewhere between an insurer of last resort and competing with the private market.

Canada's ECA, in contrast, has a commercial market orientation and is not restricted from competing with the private sector. Italy's ECA, while having to abide by EU law, also has a commercial market orientation, according to Italian officials. G-7 export credit agencies range from government agencies to private companies contracted by governments, with different organization types, governing structures, and processes for approving transactions (see table 1). The ECAs that are managed by private companies, such as those in France and Germany, experience more direct political oversight, as their governments take a more direct role in approving transactions and can take policy considerations into account on an individual transaction basis.

Ex-Im and Other G-7 ECAs Offer Different Combinations of Export Credit Support Products

G-7 ECAs each offer a different mix of export credit and other financial products. In general, a greater mix of products allows an ECA more flexibility in responding to its customers' needs, particularly during an economic crisis. Most ECAs offer standard export credit products such as export credit insurance and loan guarantees. However, ECAs may offer additional export credit products, such as direct loans (United States, Japan, and Canada) and interest make-up programs, where the ECA pays the difference between commercial lending rates and fixed OECD minimum rates (Italy, France). ECAs also may offer products that are not technically "export-related," but that, according to Ex-Im, could possibly be used in lieu of or in addition to standard export credits, such as investment insurance and untied lending. Figure 4 shows a comparison of selected export credit and other financial products offered by G-7 ECAs. Ex-Im's provision of direct loans proved to be useful during the financial crisis, when commercial financing was expensive or unavailable. While its direct lending program was little used in the early 2000s, Ex-Im experienced a surge in demand for direct loans over recent years, from $350 million in fiscal year 2008 (3 percent of its total authorizations) to $6.3 billion in fiscal year 2011 (19 percent of its total authorizations). See figure 5. The Japanese and Canadian direct loan programs also experienced increases.[11] The G-7 European ECAs, which do not have direct loan programs, sought alternative solutions to mitigate the lack of such financing.[12] Several U.S. officials and a G-7 official stated that Ex-Im's direct loan program gave it an advantage in responding to the needs of exporters and their customers during the crisis.

| | Medium- and long-term official export credits | | | | Other selected financial products | | |
| | Official financing support | | Official cover (insurance and guarantees) | | | | |
	Direct loans	Interest makeup	Export credit insurance	Loan guarantees	Working capital guarantees	Foreign investment insurance	Untied loans
United States: Ex-Im	O		O	O	O		
Canada: EDC	O			O	O	O	
France: Coface		O[a]	O	O[b]	O	O	O
Germany: Hermes PwC		O[c]	O	O[b]		O[a]	O[a]
Italy: Sace		O[a]	O	O	O	O	O
Japan: JBIC and NEXI	O		O	O		O	O
United Kingdom: ECGD			O	O	O	O	

Source: GAO analysis of ECA annual reports and discussions with ECA officials.

[a] Provided by other institutions working in concert with these ECAs.

[b] France and Germany only offer loan guarantees for exports of Airbus aircraft.

[c] Germany only offers interest make-up with regard to ECA-covered ships that have been ordered from a German shipyard.

Figure 4. Comparison of Selected Products Offered by G-7 ECAs.

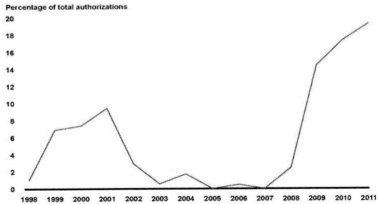

Source: GAO analysis of Ex-Im data.

Note: The percentage of total authorizations is calculated in terms of the dollar value of authorizations.

Figure 5. Ex-Im Direct Lending, 1998-2011.

EX-IM HAS SPECIFIC MANDATES AND OPERATES UNDER MORE POLICY REQUIREMENTS THAN OTHER ECAS

Ex-Im receives specific mandates from Congress and generally operates under more policy requirements than other G-7 ECAs. Ex-Im's mandates include specific targets from Congress for small business and environmentally beneficial exports. Other G-7 ECAs may have broad directives from their governments or ministries to focus on these areas. Ex-Im also faces additional mandates and legal requirements that other ECAs generally do not. For example, Ex-Im is statutorily required to perform an economic impact analysis to assess whether a project will negatively affect U.S. industries.

Ex-Im Has Specific Mandates on Small Business and Environmentally Beneficial Exports where Other G-7 ECAs Have Broad Directives

Ex-Im receives mandates from Congress that include specific targets in the areas of small business and environmentally beneficial exports, whereas some other G-7 ECAs have been given broad directives to focus on these areas by their governments or ministries. Specifically, four G-7 ECAs have received external directives to encourage small business exporters, and two ECAs have received external directives to support environmentally beneficial exports (fig. 6). According to OECD officials, Ex-Im is unique in that Congress gives it explicit policy goals to pursue in addition to its general mandate to support domestic exports. By contrast, other ECAs generally receive limited specific policy guidance from their respective legislatures and oversight ministries.

Since the 1980s, Congress has required that Ex-Im make available a certain percentage of its export financing for small business.[13] In 2002, Congress established several new requirements for Ex-Im relating to small business, including increasing the small business financing requirement from 10 to 20 percent. Related congressional directives have included requirements to create a small business division and to define standards to measure the bank's success in financing small businesses.

From fiscal years 2006 to 2010, Ex-Im met the 20 percent small business financing target, but did not in 2011. Ex-Im's small business financing percent ranged from about 27 percent in fiscal year 2007 to 18.4 percent in fiscal year 2011.[14] Because of the sharp increase in overall Ex-Im financing in 2009 and

2010, meeting the 20 percent target has meant large annual increases in small business financing. For example, Ex-Im small business financing increased by about 58 percent between 2008 and 2010.[15] According to Ex-Im officials, the bank allocates significant resources to meeting its small business mandate. About 27 staff work exclusively on small business marketing, primarily in regional offices, according to Ex-Im officials.[16]

Country	Small business	Environmentally beneficial
United States	O	O
Canada		
France	O	
Germany		
Italy		O
Japan	O	
United Kingdom	O	

Source: GAO analysis of ECA documents and interviews with ECA and government officials.

Figure 6. G-7 ECAs with External Directives to Support Small Business Exporters and Environmentally Beneficial Exports.

In 2010, Ex-Im developed and improved products to increase financing options for small business, and to simplify application processes and shorten turnaround time. For example, Ex-Im designed an express insurance product to streamline the application process for short-term export credit insurance. Other new products include ones aimed at providing competitively priced working capital finance to U.S. suppliers of U.S. exporters, and reinsurance to increase the capacity of insurance companies to offer insurance to small business exporters that have had difficulty obtaining short-term export credit since the financial crisis.

Congress also mandates Ex-Im to support environmentally beneficial exports and provides specific targets for such exports. However, specific targets in this area have greatly exceeded Ex-Im financing. In fiscal year 2008,

Congress directed Ex-Im to allocate 10 percent of its annual financing to renewable energy and environmentally beneficial products and services. For fiscal years 2009 and 2010, Congress directed Ex-Im to allocate 10 percent to a subset of those exports—renewable energy and energy efficient end-use technologies. We previously reported that Ex-Im had not come close to meeting this 10 percent target when it is applied to all of its environmentally beneficial financing.[17] Ex-Im has reported significant increases in its renewable energy financing, from $101 million in 2009 to $332 million in 2010. In 2011, Ex-Im authorized about $889 million in environmentally beneficial exports, of which about $721 million was for renewable energy.

In contrast to Ex-Im's mandates, some ECAs are broadly directed by their governments or ministries to support small business exports and environmentally beneficial exports with, generally, no specific targets to meet, according to G-7 officials. Specifically:

- The British government asks the Export Credits Guarantee Department to promote small and medium-sized exporters, but the guidance ECGD receives is suggestive, rather than a specific directive, according to officials at the ECA.
- The French Ministry of Finance provided a target for its export credit agency, Coface, to support 10,000 small and medium-sized exporters by 2012, according to Coface officials. However, officials stated that this target only applies to one product—market survey insurance—and there are many other products that Coface uses to promote exports of small businesses that are not associated with specific external targets.
- Japan's Parliament also asks JBIC to support small and medium-sized businesses, but provided a general directive to support such exporters and did not include specific targets, according to JBIC officials.
- Italy's ECA, SACE, is directed by an interministerial decree to designate renewable energy exports as a strategic sector, but no specific targets are provided, according to SACE officials.

Some ECAs that do not have external directives from their governments to support small businesses and environmentally beneficial exports have developed internal initiatives to support such exports. For example, in January 2011, Germany's ECA introduced a new product that provides a fast-tracked application process allowing exporters to receive export credit coverage for transactions of up to 5 million euros in 4 days. Additionally, Canada's ECA has developed internal initiatives to support environmentally beneficial exports. For example, a team within Export Development Canada has been tasked by EDC executives to come up with a clean technology strategy, and the team is in the early stages of putting a strategy in place, according to EDC officials.

Ex-Im Has Additional Mandates and Legal Requirements that Other ECAs Generally Do Not Have

Ex-Im has additional mandates and legal requirements that other ECAs generally do not. These include (1) promotion of exports to sub-Saharan Africa, (2) requirements to ship certain exports on U.S. flag carriers, (3) carbon policy, (4) economic impact analysis, and (5) congressional notification.[18]

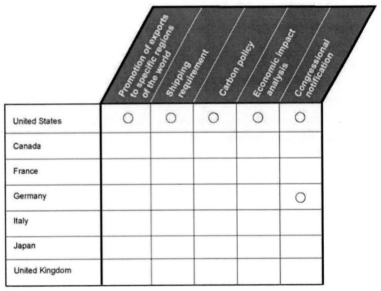

Source: GAO analysis of ECA documents and interviews with ECA and government officials.

Note: France's ECA, Coface, stated that while it does not have a specific shipping requirement, it treats shipping costs associated with shipment on non-EU vessels as foreign content.

Figure 7. G-7 ECAs with Select External Requirements.

All of these requirements, except for the carbon policy, are the result of congressional mandates. Although most ECAs do not have similar requirements (see fig. 7), as noted above, ECAs have different organizational and governance structures. These differences can affect how a government exercises policy considerations through its ECA. For example, Germany has an interministerial board that approves individual transactions and takes into account policy considerations on a case-by-case basis; in contrast, Ex-Im is an independent agency and Congress exercises policy considerations through programmatic mandates, according to a Treasury official.

Specifically, Ex-Im must consider the following mandates and legal requirements when financing transactions:

- *Promoting exports to sub-Saharan Africa.* Congress mandates that Ex-Im promote the expansion of its financial commitments in sub-Saharan Africa under Ex-Im's loan, guarantee, and insurance programs. No other G-7 ECAs have specific external requirements to support exports to sub-Saharan Africa. In 2010, Ex-Im financed 132 transactions totaling $812 million in 20 sub-Saharan African countries. Ex-Im dedicates two full-time employees to promoting exports to sub-Saharan Africa; others work part-time on the issue.

- *Requirement to ship certain exports on U.S.-flagged carriers.* Congress mandates that certain oceanborne cargo supported by U.S. government credit entities must be transported on U.S. flag vessels unless the requirement is waived by the U.S. Maritime Administration. Ex-Im interprets this legislation to mean that exports financed through its direct loan and long-term guarantee programs are subject to the U.S. flag vessel requirement.[19] In calendar year 2010, Ex-Im authorized 14 transactions valued at $2.9 billion that were subject to this requirement.

- *Carbon policy.* Ex-Im is the only G-7 ECA legally required to adopt an official carbon policy. 20 Other ECAs have adopted certain common environmental guidelines through the OECD. However, specific conditions on carbon emissions are unique to Ex-Im. Ex-Im's carbon policy, implemented in 2010, was developed in response to a lawsuit challenging Ex-Im's compliance with provisions of the National Environmental Policy Act. The carbon policy (1) promotes renewable energy exports where carbon dioxide emission levels are very low to zero, (2) establishes a $250 million facility to promote renewable energy, and (3) calls for increased transparency in the tracking and reporting of carbon dioxide emissions. In 2010, Ex-Im authorized 1 transaction valued at $887 million that was subject to the enhanced due diligence review.[21]

- *Economic impact analysis.* Congress requires Ex-Im to perform an economic impact analysis to assess whether a project will negatively affect U.S. industries either by reducing demand for goods produced in the United States or by increasing imports to the United States. Other G-7 ECAs do not have similar requirements, according to G-7 ECA officials. As we have previously reported, Ex-Im uses a screening process to identify projects with the most potential to have an adverse economic impact, and then subjects the identified projects to a detailed analysis. Of medium- and long-term transactions Ex-Im authorized in 2010, 82 transactions, valued at $2.8 billion, were subject to Ex-Im's economic impact analysis, with a small percentage of those subject to detailed analysis. [22]

- *Congressional notification.* Congress requires Ex-Im to submit a detailed statement describing and explaining a transaction to Congress prior to the Board of Directors' final approval if the transaction is (1) in an amount equal to or greater than $100,000,000 or (2) related to nuclear power or heavy water production facilities.[23] According to Hermes officials, Germany also sends a notification to the German parliament's Committee on Budgets for transactions exceeding 1 billion euros. According to Ex-Im, 38 transactions valued at about $16 billion in 2010 were sent to Congress before the Board of Directors' final approval of the transactions.

EX-IM'S DOMESTIC CONTENT REQUIREMENTS ARE GENERALLY HIGHER AND LESS FLEXIBLE THAN THOSE OF OTHER ECAS

Ex-Im's domestic content requirements are generally higher and less flexible than those of other ECAs. To fully finance a medium- or long-term transaction, Ex-Im requires that 85 percent of the value of the transaction be supplied domestically. Other G-7 ECAs generally require between zero to 51 percent domestic content. Additionally, key elements of ExIm's domestic content policy have remained relatively unchanged over two decades; at the same time, manufacturing patterns have evolved toward greater integration in production and data show that the domestic content of exports has decreased. Several ECAs have modified their policies in recent years, often citing the increasingly global content of industrial production as a primary reason for the change.

Ex-Im's Current Policy Limits the Amount of Foreign Content in the Exports It Finances

Ex-Im's domestic content policy places limits on the amount of foreign goods and services making up the exports it finances.

Domestic content refers to the portion of an exported good or service that is sourced domestically. Ex-Im's policy is not the result of a statutory requirement; according to Ex-Im, the policy reflects an attempt to balance the interests of multiple stakeholders and Ex-Im's mission to support U.S. jobs through export financing. Ex-Im's domestic content policy for medium- and longterm transactions limits its level of support to the lesser of (1) 85 percent of the total value of all eligible goods and services in the U.S. export transaction,[24] or (2) 100 percent of the U.S. content in all eligible goods and services in the U.S. export transaction.[25]

In effect, Ex-Im requires 85 percent domestic content to receive full financing for medium- and longterm transactions but does not require a minimum amount of domestic content to receive a *portion* of financing. See the sidebar for two examples of how the domestic content policy affects the level of support Ex-Im can provide.

Ex-Im has separate domestic content requirements for short-term transactions—the percentage required to receive maximum coverage is lower than for medium- and long-term transactions and the calculation method differs.

The short-term policy is generally more lenient for small businesses than for other exporters. For example, small businesses can satisfy the short-term domestic content requirement based on aggregating all of the products in an export contract, while non-small businesses must meet the minimum domestic content threshold on a product-by-product basis. In addition, small businesses include indirect costs in the calculation of domestic content.[26]

According to Ex-Im, the difference reflects Ex-Im's directive to consider the unique business requirements of small businesses.

Examples Illustrating Ex-Im's Medium- and Long-Term Domestic Content Policy

Ex-Im's domestic content policy determines the total level of support it can provide for medium- and long-term transactions by providing the lesser of

(1)   85 percent of the value of all eligible goods and services in the contract. For example,

A U.S. exporter is selling manufacturing equipment to Mexico in a contract worth $10 million. Of the $10 million contract, $9 million is U.S. content and the remaining $1 million is foreign content. Thus,

$9/$10 x 100 = 90 percent, which is equal to or greater than 85 percent

Therefore, the contract is eligible for 85 percent financing.

(2)   100 percent of the U.S. content of all eligible goods and services in the contract. For example,

A U.S. exporter is selling manufacturing equipment to Mexico in a contract worth $10 million. Of the $10 million contract, $7.5 million is U.S. content and the remaining $2.5 million is foreign content. Thus,

$7.5/$10 x 100 = 75 percent, which is less than 85 percent.

Therefore, only the U.S. content is eligible for financing, so the exporter would receive 75 percent financing

Other ECAs Generally Have Lower and More Flexible Domestic Content Requirements than Ex-Im

Other G-7 ECAs have lower domestic content requirements than Ex-Im, generally requiring between zero and 51 percent domestic content (see table 2). Some ECAs with domestic content polices have more flexibility in implementing their policies by allowing for exceptions to their minimum domestic content requirements on a transaction-by-transaction basis. For example, according to Japanese officials, Japan's ECAs require a minimum of 30 percent domestic content, but the institutions can make exceptions for projects deemed to be of strategic importance. Ex-Im makes no exceptions to its content policy for specific transactions, except for those involving tied aid or raw materials.[27] According to Canadian and Italian officials, Canada and Italy do not require a certain level of domestic content; rather, both consider domestic content in the context of a broad range of factors to determine whether supporting a transaction benefits national interest.

Table 2. Domestic Content Policies of the G-7 ECAs, Including Minimum Domestic Content to Receive Full Medium- and Long-Term Support

Country	Domestic content policies of the G-7 ECAs, for medium- and long-term support
United States	Eighty-five percent domestic content requirement to receive full financing. If less than 85 percent, Ex-Im will finance the domestic content portion.
Canada	No minimum domestic content requirement. National Benefits policy first considers the gross domestic product and employmentimpacts of the transaction and then takes into account other factors, such as increased access to global markets.
France	Twenty percent domestic content requirement for a transaction to be considered.a
Germany	Three-tier policy: 70 percent and 51 percent minimum domestic content for the first two tiers, respectively. For the third tier, transactions with less than 51 percent domestic content can be supported if there is a justification from the exporter and Interministerial Committee approval.b
Italy	No minimum domestic content requirement. The ECA supports exports that benefit the Italian economy and has internal considerations, such as a maximum exposure amount for a country. If the ECA is close to reaching this amount, it will try to maximize Italian content in the export.
Japan	Thirty percent domestic content requirement. The ECA can make exceptions to support projects with less than 30 percent domestic content if the project has strategic interests.
United Kingdom	Twenty percent domestic content requirement to receive full support. If less than 20 percent, the ECA will support the domesticcontent portion of the transaction.

Source: GAO analysis of ECA documents and interviews with officials.

Notes: ECAs from six of the seven G-7 countries, including the United States, stated that they calculate domestic content as a percentage of the total value of the export contract. They also stated that the domestic content amount is self-reported, or generally self-reported, by applicants. This table does not reflect differences in ECA policies for supporting local costs, which can affect the amount of foreign content supported in some transactions. Local costs are for goods and services manufactured or originated in the buyer's country.

[a]French officials stated that going below 50 percent involves some restrictions.

[b]The second-tier level requires between 70 to 51 percent domestic content in certain situations, such as when the foreign content comes from EU countries, Switzerland, Japan, or Norway and at the same time from a third country; when it comes from German subsidiaries not located in the buyer's country; or certain other situations. With respect to the third tier, according to German officials, support of such transactions is done on a limited basis.

EDC's Canadian Benefits policy considers the research and development spending by the company and the potential for increased access to global markets, among other factors, when deciding to finance a transaction (see textbox). According to Canadian officials, the Canadian Benefits model is designed to capture all benefits that accrue from Canadian companies' involvement in international trade.

In the early 2000s, Export Development Canada implemented a national benefits policy rather than a domestic content requirement, referred to as the Canadian Benefits model. With this model, EDC measures its contribution to Canada's economy through the economic benefits generated by the exports and investments it supports. EDC takes the following steps under the Canadian Benefits model:

1. *Calculate economic benefits.* The economic benefits are based on the amount of gross domestic product (GDP) in the exports it finances by determining the amount of Canadian content in the export. The Canadian content is provided by Statistics Canada's Input/Output Model, which tracks the production chain of Canadian industries, and identifies and measures inputs and outputs.
2. *Calculate base grade.* EDC then calculates a base grade by dividing the level of GDP generated by the transaction by the amount of EDC support that was requested. EDC assigns letter grades A-F according to these support percentages.
3. *Identify upgrades.* Where a transaction generates a base grade of less than B, additional benefits are considered in order to upgrade the transaction. Each applicable secondary benefit boosts the base grade by one letter grade. (An F rating cannot receive upgrades.) Reasons for upgrades include the following:

- Above average research and development spending by the Canadian company.
- The transaction allows increased access to global markets.
- The transaction has an above average employment impact.
- The Canadian exporter is a small or medium-sized business.
- The transaction supports an environmentally beneficial product.

Although transactions rarely receive low final grades, low grades do not prevent EDC from financing the transaction, according to EDC officials.

In addition to the domestic content policies presented in table 2, ECAs' policies for supporting local costs can also affect the level of support they can provide related to goods and services that are not sourced domestically. Local costs are for goods and services manufactured or originated in the buyer's country, such as on-site construction costs. ExIm's policy allows it to support up to 30 percent of the value of the export contract in local costs, in addition to 15 percent foreign content.[28]

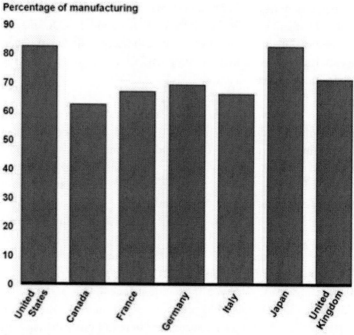

Source: GAO analysis of OECD data.

Note: OECD uses input-output tables from each country to estimate the domestic content of exports. An input-output table is a means of presenting a detailed analysis of the process of production and the use of goods and services (products) and the income generated in that production. An input-output table shows the inputs that are used by each industry, including imports, to produce its output, the output of each industry, and the use of outputs of various industries by final consumers. Input-output analysis can be used to study changes in the structure of an economy.

Figure 8. Domestic Content Share of Manufacturing Exports among G-7 Countries, 2005.

In contrast, according to Ex-Im, the other G-7 ECAs generally include local costs in their calculation of foreign content, and this can reduce the gap between the level of foreign content that Ex-Im can support and that of its foreign counterparts. Ex-Im reported that, in 2010, 21 percent of its non-aircraft medium- and long-term transactions contained some local cost support.

The degree to which countries rely on domestic components in producing its exports differs. U.S. exports generally have higher domestic content than those of other G-7 countries. OECD data show that domestic content accounts for less than 75 percent of manufacturing exports for five of the seven G-7 countries, but accounts for over 80 percent of manufacturing exports for the United States, as well as in Japan.

While Ex-Im Has Modified Its Method for Calculating Domestic Content, Its Threshold for Receiving Full Financing Has Not Changed since 1987

While Ex-Im has modified its method for calculating the amount of domestic content in a transaction, its minimum threshold for receiving full financing for medium- and long-term transactions has not changed since 1987. Before 1987, Ex-Im financed only the domestic portion of medium- and long-term transactions. If less than 100 percent of an export's content was domestic, the foreign part would be carved out and Ex-Im would finance 85 percent of the domestic portion.[29] In 1987, Ex-Im adopted its current policy to allow transactions with up to 15 percent foreign content to receive 85 percent of the total contract value. Ex-Im's rationale for allowing up to 15 percent foreign content was that the 15 percent down payment required by the OECD Arrangement would cover the portion of foreign content, according to Ex-Im officials.

In 2001, Ex-Im modified its method of calculating the domestic content of exports in medium- and long-term transactions. Previously, Ex-Im required exporters to report the domestic content of individual items in a contract, line by line. In 2001, Ex-Im moved to a whole contract value calculation where exporters report the domestic content of the contract's entire value, rather than item by item. This allowed Ex-Im to finance contracts that may have individual items that contain less than 85 percent domestic content as long as the total amount in the contract has 85 percent or more domestic content.

There have not been subsequent changes to the policy for medium- and long-term transactions.

Domestic Content of U.S. Exports Has Generally Declined and Varies across Sectors

Production patterns have changed in the past few decades as global manufacturing has become more integrated. Companies increasingly rely on parts sourced from other countries, and as a result, the domestic content in exported goods has declined.

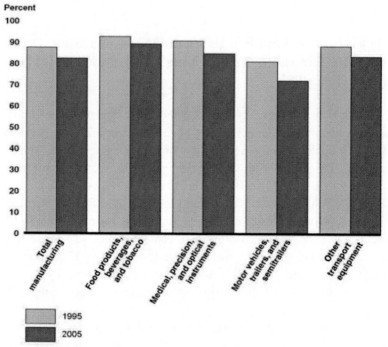

Source: GAO analysis of OECD data.
Note: The data are reported in 5-year intervals because of the availability of input-output tables for most countries. The most recent year for which OECD did this analysis is 2005. U.S. input-output tables use data collected every 5 years in an Economic Census done by the U.S. Census Bureau. "Other transport equipment" covers aircraft, a major product supported by Ex-Im financing.

Figure 9. Domestic Content of Select U.S. Exports, 1995 to 2005.

OECD data show that from 1995 to 2005 the percentage of domestic content of manufactured U.S. exports declined from 87.4 percent to 82.4 percent, a 5 percentage point decline in 10 years (see fig. 9). Ex-Im does not differentiate among sectors in its domestic content policy, although domestic content in U.S. exports varies by sector. Among manufactured exports, medical, precision and optical instruments showed a greater decline in domestic content, almost 6 percentage points, than food products, beverages, and tobacco, which experienced a 3.6 percentage point decrease. As figure 9 shows, as of 2005, the domestic content of U.S. exports of motor vehicles, trailers, and semitrailers was around 72 percent, and other transportation equipment, which includes aircraft, was 83.5 percent.

Given varying levels of domestic content by product and industry, Ex-Im may be unable to provide full financing for exports in certain industries if trends continue. Domestic content in Ex-Im transactions fluctuated from 1997 to 2010, showing an overall downward trend. The average domestic content for medium- and long-term transactions containing foreign content was 91 percent in 1997 and 86 percent in 2010 (see figure 10).

This value is near the 85 percent minimum domestic content required for a transaction to receive full Ex-Im financing.

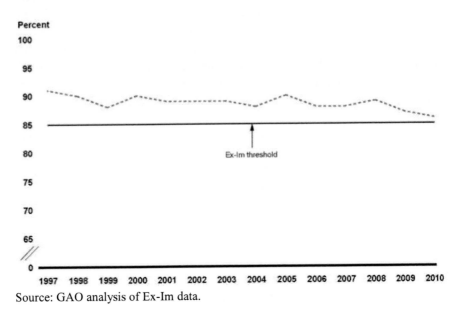

Source: GAO analysis of Ex-Im data.

Figure 10. Average Domestic Content for Ex-Im's Medium- and Long-term Transactions Containing Foreign Content, 1997 through 2010.

Concerns about Ex-Im's Content Policy Exist among Exporters and Lenders

Exporters and lenders have expressed concerns about Ex-Im's policy, although obtaining clear evidence about the policy's impact is difficult. In cases where domestic content falls below 85 percent, Ex-Im's policy could potentially have a negative impact on U.S. competitiveness by deterring exporters from using Ex-Im's products. According to respondents of Ex-Im's most recent survey concerning its competitiveness, Ex-Im's content policy is the bank's most significant impediment to competitiveness.[30]

Exporters have urged Ex-Im to expand its criteria for support beyond domestic content and to consider support based on national interests.

Exporters and lenders have also suggested that Ex-Im should explore extending exceptions to its content policy to support priority sectors, such as environmentally beneficial projects.

According to Ex-Im officials, information on exporters that have not applied for Ex-Im financing because of its domestic content policy or deals that have been lost as a result of incomplete financing is not tracked. Co-financing is a tool that some exporters can use to address financing challenges posed by domestic content requirements, but it is not available for all transactions.

Co-financing arrangements allow an exporter to offer a single ECA support package to a buyer interested in procuring products from two or more countries. The G-7 ECAs have multiple framework agreements that govern co-financing among themselves. Ex-Im officials stated that co-financing is increasingly used in situations where foreign content exceeds 15 percent and there is a gap in Ex-Im's financing coverage. In 2010, Ex-Im co-financed more than $6.5 billion in transactions, with the vast majority of transactions involving aircraft. However, co-financing is not an option for all U.S. transactions, because it requires meeting the financing requirement of another country's ECA, particularly the production of a product or service that would qualify as an export from that country.

Other ECAs Have Modified Their Domestic Content Policies to Reflect Changing Global Production Patterns

Some ECAs have revised their domestic content policies to reflect changes in global production patterns. For example, following an evaluation

10 years ago, EDC and the Canadian government determined that EDC's 50 percent domestic content rule had become onerous, and that the global marketplace had changed, with more production involving foreign content, according to Canadian officials. EDC adopted an "integrative trade model" to reflect multiple benefits brought to Canada from international transactions. As a result, EDC moved to the National Benefits policy discussed above, where exporters using little or no domestic content are eligible for support, as long as their export is determined to benefit Canada.

According to UK officials, ECGD also substantially changed its policy in 2007, determining that its domestic content requirement of 60 percent was an artificial barrier and unnecessary restriction, in light of declines in the size of the UK manufacturing base, increased globalization, and multisourcing of goods under UK export contracts. It lowered the requirement to 20 percent. In 2008, Germany moved from a 90 percent domestic content requirement to its current three-tier policy that attaches various limits to differing levels of domestic content.

Germany's federal government made these changes in response to the repeated appeals of German exporters, who increasingly viewed the previous system as overly restrictive in light of international competition, according to Hermes documents and officials. There are differing views on the ultimate impact of different domestic content requirements, and limited analytical evidence on which to base decisions is available. While lowering a domestic content requirement can increase the number and type of transactions that an ECA can support, it could lessen the incentive for some companies seeking ECA support to source goods and services domestically.

The potential impact on U.S. employment of any changes in the policy would depend on the balance of job gains that might accrue from supporting additional transactions against any job losses from reduced domestic content. As other ECAs have loosened their domestic content policies, Ex-Im's policy remains relatively unchanged. Congress directs Ex-Im to provide financing that is fully competitive with the financing of its competitors.[31]

According to Ex-Im officials, Ex-Im reviews its domestic content policy on a regular basis to identify ways to increase flexibilities for exporters. However, Ex-Im has not conducted a systematic review of its policy in recent years to assess to what extent the overall impact of the policy is consistent with Ex-Im's mission of supporting U.S. jobs.

THE OECD ARRANGEMENT HAS DECREASED EXPORT CREDIT SUBSIDIES, BUT THE INCREASING IMPORTANCE OF NONMEMBERS THREATENS ITS FUTURE EFFECTIVENESS

While the scope of the OECD Arrangement has expanded to cover additional aspects of officially supported export credit terms among member ECAs, the increasing activities of nonmembers, particularly China, threaten the future ability of the agreement to provide a level playing field for exporters. Several agreements establish guidelines for pricing and reporting on export credit support. However, these agreements apply only to officially supported activities of participant ECAs. Several countries, including Brazil, China, and India, have growing ECA financing activity but are not part of the Arrangement. Officials from several G-7 ECAs and other institutions identify engagement with these countries to increase transparency and promote broader discussion of export credit issues as a major challenge that must be addressed if the Arrangement is to remain effective.

The OECD Arrangement Has Expanded over Time to Regulate Additional Aspects of Official ECA Support

The scope of the OECD Arrangement has expanded over time to regulate additional aspects of participating countries' use of officially supported export credits, decreasing export subsidies in the process. Since the Arrangement was formed, in 1978, there have been several important agreements among member countries that have regulated pricing or other aspects of export credit support. These agreements include the following:

- *Minimum interest rates.* Arrangement members adopted a system of minimum interest rates, which has reduced the interest rate subsidy component in ECA support. These rates, called Commercial Interest Reference Rates (CIRR), are adjusted on a monthly basis to reflect commercial lending rates for borrowers in the domestic market of the relevant currency.
- *Minimum premium rates (risk fees).* Agreements on minimum premium rates, or risk fees, are designed to encourage convergence in pricing, further decreasing opportunities for subsidies among ECAs.

The first agreement on risk-based premium rates, in 1997, established a set of minimum premium rates to reflect country credit risk. Countries were free to charge higher rates than these minimums. A new agreement, effective as of September 2011, expanded on this earlier agreement by including buyer credit (commercial), as well as country-based, aspects of risk. This agreement reduces ECAs' flexibility in pricing commercial transactions, thus further narrowing differences in ECA financing terms.

- *Tied aid.* Two agreements have restricted the use of tied aid, that is, aid conditioned on the purchase of goods and services from the donor country. In 1987, Arrangement members agreed to raise the minimum concessionality level for tied aid permitted under the Arrangement to 35 percent.[32] In 1991, a further agreement prohibited tied and partially untied aid to richer developing countries, as well as for projects that were considered commercially viable.
- *Sector agreements.* Sector agreements have been reached for civil aircraft, nuclear power plants, renewable energies and water projects, and ships. Some of these agreements have different rules for minimum interest and premium rates and maximum repayments terms than those that apply to standard transactions through the Arrangement. The Aircraft Sector Understanding is especially significant because it regulates aircraft support terms for ECAs of major aircraft-exporting countries, including the United States, Brazil, Canada, France, Germany, and the United Kingdom. A large share of some countries' ECA support is in the aircraft sector.

The Arrangement also has a variety of reporting requirements in conjunction with its overall and sector agreements that provide transparency about ECA activities to Arrangement members. ECAs must report all of their long-term officially supported export credit transactions to the OECD as they occur and, twice a year, report the amount of outstanding officially supported export credits. Further, separate reporting requirements apply with respect to minimum premium rates as well as the aircraft sector agreement. OECD officials said they are hoping to streamline these reporting requirements and are in the process of approving a new data-reporting directive.[33]

However, certain export credit transactions of member ECAs fall outside the Arrangement and its reporting requirements, which lessens the transparency of ECA activities. These include "market windows," or support that an ECA provides on market terms. Canada's ECA currently provides this type of support.[34] The use of market windows has historically been an issue of concern for the United States, because of limited transparency and the potential for unfair advantage stemming from an ECA's government connection.[35]

A second type of transaction outside the scope of the Arrangement is non-export credit financing activities, such as untied lending and investment finance. A majority of G-7 ECAs offer untied lending, which takes the form of loans extended to other countries for strategic reasons. While these loans are not directly linked to the purchase of exports from the lending country, the terms can take whatever form the two countries agree upon. For instance, Japan provided an untied loan to a commercial bank in Malaysia in order to provide long-term financing to Japanese companies located there, as well as local companies within their supply chain. Ex-Im officials have expressed concern about the growing use of this financing tool because of its potential linkage to exports and uncertainty about how its utilization could affect Ex-Im.

Export Credits from Countries Outside the OECD Arrangement Are Increasing

Official export credits from emerging economies such as China, India, and Brazil have experienced rapid growth. As nonparticipants in the OECD Arrangement, these countries can offer terms more favorable than terms under the Arrangement.[36] More favorable terms to buyers do not necessarily constitute subsidies—the terms may be market-based and compliant with World Trade Organization requirements—but can be more generous than those allowed by the Arrangement, according to Ex-Im. However, since these countries are exempt from the Arrangement's requirement to report each transaction, there is uncertainty regarding the terms that they offer.

As total exports from emerging economies have increased, so have their officially supported export credits. From 2006 to 2010, total exports from China, India, and Brazil increased over 60 percent, while medium- and long-term official export credits for China and Brazil are estimated to have more than doubled—and for India nearly doubled—during the same time period (see fig. 11). China is now estimated to be the largest supplier of medium- and long-term export credits.[37] Ex-Im estimated that China offered $45 billion in official medium- and long-term export credits in 2010, twice as much as Germany, the largest provider among G-7 ECAs.

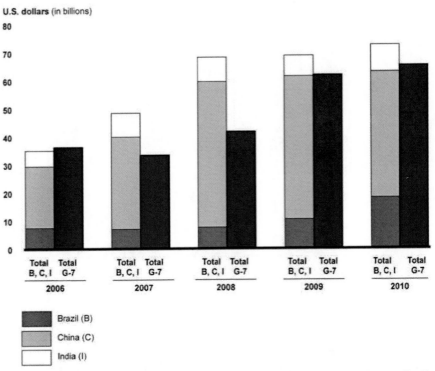

U.S. dollars (in billions)

Brazil (B)
China (C)
India (I)

Source: GAO analysis of data from Report to the U.S. Congress on Export Credit Competition and the Export-Import Bank of the United States, period January 2010-December 2010.

Note: Data represent the medium- and long-term officially supported export credits issued each year by country. Ex-Im notes the difficulties in obtaining comparable data from non-OECD ECAs because of the lack of information. Ex-Im used a variety of methods to collect and estimate the export credit volumes. Ex-Im notes that the figures for China, Brazil, and India likely overstate these countries' activities.

Figure 11. Estimated Medium- and Long-Term Official Export Credits, 2006-2010.

According to China Ex-Im Bank annual reports, it provided more than $36 billion in total export credit support in 2010, more than five times the $4 billion provided in 2000. India's Ex-Im Bank experienced similar growth, increasing its activities from about $500 million in 2000 to $11 billion in 2010. Over the same time period, U.S. Ex-Im's financing increased from about $13 billion to $24.5 billion. Figure 12 compares the activities and relative growth of the Export-Import Banks of China, India, and the United States.

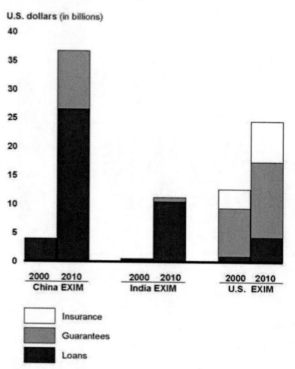

Source: GAO estimates based on annual reports from China, India, and U.S. Export-
Import Banks.

Notes: The loans from China Ex-Im Bank include seller and buyer credits. Seller credit
is broadly defined as a line of credit and can be extended either in China's
currency, the renminbi, or foreign currencies. China Ex-Im Bank provides these
credits to Chinese enterprises for financing their construction projects
implemented in foreign countries, which may support the export of Chinese
equipment, machinery, building materials, technology, and labor services.
According to U.S. Ex-Im, the buyer credit offered by China Ex-Im Bank is the
most similar to the type of transaction-specific long-term support made available
by the G-7 ECAs.

China Ex-Im Bank reports the amount disbursed while U.S. Ex-Im and India Ex-Im
report the amount committed.

Dollar amounts shown are in nominal terms.

Figure 12. Estimated Activity Levels for Export-Import Banks of China, India, and the
United States, 2000 and 2010.

SINOSURE, China's other ECA, also has experienced sharp growth.
SINOSURE stated in its 2010 annual report that it underwrote an aggregate

amount of $196.4 billion for that year, an increase of 68.5 percent over 2009. This follows a growth of 85.8 percent from 2008 to 2009.

Given the increase in China's officially supported export credits, officials from some G-7 countries have expressed interest in additional information about the terms and volume of China's activities, but officials reported that obtaining such information is difficult. Some information on total volume of export credits is provided through annual reports, but in limited detail. As discussed above, China's position outside the OECD Arrangement limits its reporting requirements relative to G-7 ECAs. Thus, determining the nature of its activities and the extent to which financing terms (in contrast to other factors, such as production cost) are the key reason for Chinese companies' securing deals is difficult. An expert on China reported having obtained information on China's export financing activities from recipient countries rather than from China. In addition, officials from several G-7 countries told us that they obtain anecdotal information on China's activities from their exporters, who may be facing Chinese competition. One OECD official expressed the view that China will become more competitive with the G-7 ECAs over the next 10 years as the technology differential between Chinese and G-7 exports decreases.

Engagement with China and Other Emerging Economies Presents Challenges for the OECD Arrangement

According to officials from the OECD and several G-7 ECAs, engagement with emerging economies, especially China, on practices related to export credit financing is increasingly important and presents challenges for the OECD Arrangement and its participants. A senior OECD official stated that the rise of this export financing competition threatens the Arrangement's ability to maintain a level playing field among exporting nations.

Various ECAs, governments, and the OECD have made efforts to engage China on export credit issues, including encouraging participation in various forums, but have generally reported limited success. For example, Canadian officials reported encouraging their Chinese counterparts to join multilateral forums. Japanese officials said they reach out to Chinese officials on a regular basis, including at meetings among Asian ECAs. U.S. Treasury officials noted that export credits were mentioned at the U.S.-China Strategic and Economic Dialogue, a high-level forum between U.S. and Chinese government officials. They also reported that OECD and country officials have made attempts to invite China to export credit-related meetings. However, several ECA, government and OECD officials reported that China is often unwilling to attend or sends lower-level representatives to these meetings, such as a recent G-20 meeting in Paris.

In some cases, an ECA in an emerging economy will see an incentive to joining international agreements or institutions. In 2004, Brazil participated in the negotiations on the Aircraft Sector Understanding and in 2007 joined the actual agreement. One U.S. official points to Brazil's interest in obtaining information on Canada, its primary competitor, and a desire to help shape the rules, as strong incentives that brought it to the negotiating table. Another institution, the Berne Union, which is an association of export credit and investment insurance providers, has a broad base of membership, including some of the ECAs from China, India, and Brazil. Through membership, they have agreed to follow certain principles, including a pledge not to subsidize exports. This institution may provide an additional venue by which these emerging economies can be engaged in discussions concerning export support and related issues. However, some ECA and other officials point to China's current lack of incentive to engage. OECD and other officials have stressed to China one benefit of joining the Arrangement now: the opportunity to shape the rules by which their competitors must abide.

CONCLUSION

Established with a mission to support U.S. jobs and an explicit charge to provide export financing competitive with that of other governments, ExIm is expected to play a key role in increasing U.S. exports, be self-sustaining in terms of its budget, and fulfill a number of policy directives beyond those of other G-7 ECAs. In terms of its volume of export credit support, Ex-Im's performance in recent years has been quite strong; the bank's total authorizations have increased steadily as demand for its services has been high during a period of global financial turmoil. Whether Ex-Im will see an increasing tension across its mission and requirements remains to be seen, but there is some evidence of that now, as the bank's small business financing share for fiscal year 2011 was below its 20 percent target for the first time in 5 years. Although small business financing grew in 2011, it grew less than Ex-Im's overall financing.

Ex-Im's domestic content requirement for receiving full medium- and long- term financing, which Ex-Im determines, is generally higher than that of other ECAs and less flexible. While other ECAs have loosened their domestic content policies in recent years, key elements of Ex-Im's policy remain relatively unchanged. Ex-Im officials state that Ex-Im's policy reflects its attempt to balance the interests of multiple stakeholders and its mission to support U.S. jobs. However, to what extent Ex-Im's current policy affects its support of U.S. jobs is not clear-cut. It may provide an incentive for certain exporters to buy from U.S. suppliers. On the other hand, to the degree that the requirement limits the ability of a larger number of exporters to obtain full Ex-Im financing, it may deter foreign buyers from sourcing from U.S. firms. Given these factors, and trends toward increasing global economic production, a better understanding of how Ex-Im's policy may affect U.S. exporters and jobs is needed.

Strong increases in export financing by several emerging countries present competitive challenges that Ex-Im alone cannot readily address. The OECD Arrangement has made important strides toward decreasing subsidies in export credits and leveling the playing field for exporters. However, emerging economies with rapidly growing export credit support levels that are outside the Arrangement are exempt from its reporting requirements and rules and can offer terms that are more generous than parties to the Arrangement can. Member countries have taken some steps within the OECD and beyond it to engage countries including Brazil, China, and India on export credit issues. However, some acknowledge that China is not currently motivated to join any type of agreement. There is concern that, in particular, the rise of China's export financing threatens the Arrangement's ability to support a level playing field among exporting nations.

RECOMMENDATIONS FOR EXECUTIVE ACTION

To maintain Ex-Im's competitiveness and enhance its ability to support U.S. exports, we recommend that the Ex-Im Bank conduct a systematic review of its domestic content policy in the context of changing production patterns to ensure this policy effectively serves the objective of creating U.S. jobs while also providing financing that is competitive with that of other ECAs.

To preserve and enhance the competitiveness of U.S. exports and to promote transparency, we recommend that the Secretary of the Treasury, in conjunction with Ex-Im and working with international counterparts, develop strategies to further encourage and increase engagement of emerging economy countries in discussions and agreements on export credit support.

AGENCY COMMENTS AND OUR EVALUATION

Ex-Im and Treasury provided comments on a draft of this report. In its written comments, Ex-Im stated that GAO's findings are generally consistent with Ex-Im's findings in its 2010 Competitiveness Report and that the lack of transparency from non-OECD ECAs is the major challenge to a level playing field globally. Ex-Im did not directly address GAO's recommendation that it conduct a systematic review of its domestic content policy and its impacts but stated that it disagreed with GAO's characterization of how Ex-Im has addressed the issue of domestic content. Treasury provided a statement concerning its full support of engaging market economy countries on export credit issues, but did not state whether it agreed or disagreed with our recommendation.

With respect to its domestic content policy, Ex-Im stated that the policy should be considered in light of Ex-Im's specific mandate to focus on jobs. Our report emphasizes that Ex-Im's explicit mandate to support U.S. jobs is unique among G-7 ECAs. In addition, the report states that ExIm's policy is the result of an attempt to balance the interests of multiple stakeholders with its mission to support U.S. jobs through export financing.

Ex-Im also stated that its co-financing and local cost policies are important in evaluating the competitiveness of its domestic content policies. In discussing foreign content policy, our report acknowledges the role of co-financing as a tool for some exporters, and explicitly notes that Ex-Im provided more than $6.5 billion for co-financing in 2010. With respect to local cost, we agree that the treatment of local cost financing is relevant to the discussion of foreign content, and we have added related information to the report.

Ex-Im stated it disagrees with the report's characterization of how Ex-Im has addressed the issue of content, stating that it has regularly reviewed the policy as part of its annual competitiveness report, and has made changes. We do not believe that Ex-Im's competitiveness reports constitute the systematic review of the content policy recommended in our report, and we maintain that a more comprehensive review, including its impact on U.S. jobs, is needed. Ex-Im's competitiveness reports have consistently identified its content policy as a major competitive barrier, with Ex-Im stating in its latest report, published in June 2011, that "Ex-Im Bank's content requirements and implementation of those requirements are significantly more restrictive than those of its G-7 counterparts" and that "in cases where foreign content exceeds 15 percent Ex-Im Bank's policy and practice can have a negative impact on U.S.

competitiveness because it may deter exporters from using Ex-Im's products."
Ex-Im reported that its exporters and lenders identified foreign content as their
"most significant impediment to competitiveness." In terms of changes made
to Ex-Im's policy over time, our report states that Ex-Im last changed its level
of minimum domestic content required for receiving full financing for
medium- and long-term transactions (85 percent) in 1987 and in 2001 changed
its method for calculating the percentage of domestic content in a transaction.
The report also clearly lays out Ex-Im's content policy for short-term
financing, including specific provisions for small businesses. We have
clarified summary language regarding what aspects of the policy have not
changed since 1987. Ex-Im also provided technical comments, which we
incorporated as appropriate.

Treasury provided the following response: "Treasury fully supports and
encourages emerging market economy countries with major medium/long-
term export credit programs to join in discussions and agreements on export
credit support, and is actively engaged in that endeavor." We describe in the
report that member countries, including the United States, have taken some
steps within the OECD and beyond it to engage emerging market economy
countries on export credit issues, and that the issue of export credits was raised
at the U.S.-China Strategic and Economic Dialogue, a high-level forum
between U.S. and Chinese government officials, including the Treasury
Secretary. However, we believe it is important that Treasury take further steps
to encourage and increase engagement of these countries on export credit
issues. We slightly modified the wording of the recommendation to reflect
this.

Loren Yager
Managing Director, International Affairs and Trade

APPENDIX I: OBJECTIVES, SCOPE, AND METHODOLOGY

The objectives of this report were to examine (1) Ex-Im's mission,
organization, market orientation, and product offerings compared with those of
other Group of Seven (G-7) export credit agencies (ECAs), (2) Ex-Im's policy
requirements compared with those of other G-7 ECAs, (3) Ex-Im's domestic
content policy compared with those of the other G-7 ECAs, and (4) the role of
the Organisation for Economic Cooperation and Development (OECD)
Arrangement in governing ECA activities.

To assess how Ex-Im's mission, organization, market orientation, and product offerings compared with those of other G-7 ECAs, we reviewed relevant documents, including ECA annual reports and other publications, such as Ex-Im's annual Competitiveness Reports, OECD reports, and legislation authorizing various ECAs. We also reviewed ECAs' websites for additional information regarding product offerings. We interviewed officials from each of the G-7 ECAs and government organizations that have oversight over the ECAs. These organizations included Ex-Im in the United States; Export Development Canada (EDC), Department of Foreign Affairs and International Trade and Department of Finance in Canada; Coface and the Ministry of Economy, Finance and Industry in France; Euler Hermes, PricewaterhouseCoopers and the Interministerial Council, represented by the Federal Ministry of Economics and Technology, in Germany; Servizi Assicurativi del Commercio Estero (SACE) and the Ministry of Economic Development in Italy; Japan Bank for International Cooperation (JBIC) and Nippon Export and Investment Insurance (NEXI) (via telephone) in Japan; and the Export Credits Guarantee Department (ECGD) in the United Kingdom. We also interviewed officials from the U.S. Departments of Treasury and State, as well as the OECD and the Berne Union. In addition, we spoke with several institutions that work in conjunction with official ECAs: Societa Italiana per le Imprese all'Estero (SIMEST) in Italy and KfW IPEX-Bank in Germany.

To assess how Ex-Im's policy requirements compared with those of the other G-7 ECAs, we first examined Ex-Im's policy requirements by reviewing Ex-Im annual reports; Ex-Im Competitiveness Reports; Ex-Im' 2010-2015 Strategic Plan; GAO reports on Ex-Im's small business mandate, environmentally beneficial mandate, and economic impact analysis requirement;[1] Congressional Research Service (CRS) reports; testimony from congressional hearings; and academic articles. We also interviewed Ex-Im officials to talk about the various policy requirements, and we interviewed officials from the Small Business Administration (SBA) to discuss Ex-Im's small business mandate. To examine the other G-7 ECAs' policy requirements and how they compared with those of ExIm, we interviewed officials from the G-7 ECAs, as well as any government organizations that play an oversight role for these ECAs. We asked them directly whether they shared any of Ex-Im's policy requirements, and more generally, whether they had other policy requirements, such as requirements to focus on promoting certain types of exports, export destinations, or exporters, and whether this resulted from external directives or internal decisions. We also asked about the nature of their relationships with oversight organizations and the extent to which they received external policy guidance from these organizations or their legislatures. In cases where ECA officials told us that there was legislation that authorized or otherwise governed their activities, and there were English versions available, we reviewed this legislation. We also reviewed ECA annual reports. We sent follow-up questions to all of the ECAs to confirm the information they had given us during interviews regarding their policy requirements. We also provided ECAs the opportunity to provide technical comments on portions of the report that contain information pertaining to the ECA.

To examine how Ex-Im's domestic content policy compares with those of other G-7 ECAs, we first collected information on Ex-Im's policy from its competitiveness reports and website. We reviewed testimony transcripts from congressional hearings and literature on domestic content of exports and global manufacturing production patterns. We also interviewed Ex-Im officials responsible for administering the policy, as well as officials at the Treasury Department and the Coalition for Employment through Exports, an advocacy organization on matters affecting U.S. government export finance. To obtain information on other G-7 ECAs' domestic content policies, we reviewed their annual reports. We interviewed G-7 ECA officials, who explained their policies and provided additional documentation. We analyzed global manufacturing production trends using OECD data on the foreign content of the United States' and other countries' exports by sector, from the mid-1990s to the mid-2000s. To assess the reliability of the OECD data, we reviewed the data documentation, tested for internal consistency of the data, and compared the trends with other sources. We found that the data were sufficiently reliable for the purposes of presenting global manufacturing trends, demonstrating country and sector variances. We collected data from ExIm on the percentage of foreign content in the exports it finances. Ex-Im reports this data annually in its Competitiveness Report. We found that the data were sufficiently reliable for the purposes of presenting the amount of foreign versus domestic content in exports it finances.

To analyze the role of the OECD Arrangement in governing ECA activities, we reviewed the text of the OECD Arrangement as well as a variety of OECD and other reports on the Arrangement, Export Credit Group, and export credit activities. We interviewed OECD officials, as well as G-7 ECA officials, to discuss the history and evolving role of the Arrangement as well as current challenges. We conducted a literature search and reviewed academic literature on the Arrangement and ECAs. To obtain information on China's export credit activities, we met with U.S. Treasury and State Department officials in Washington and Beijing and interviewed experts, including academic experts at American University and the Brookings Institution. We also discussed China's activities with G7 ECA and other officials. To obtain data on China's, India's, and Brazil's ECA activities, we reviewed information from the International Monetary Fund, ECA annual reports, and Ex-Im's 2010 Competitiveness Report. We also used data published in the annual reports from China's and India's Ex-Im Banks to compare the growth of export financing from China and India to that of the U.S. Ex-Im Bank. We found the data were sufficiently reliable for the purpose of comparing levels of growth.

We conducted this performance audit from February 2011 to February 2012 in accordance with generally accepted government auditing standards. Those standards require that we plan and perform the audit to obtain sufficient, appropriate evidence to provide a reasonable basis for our findings and conclusions based on our audit objectives. We believe that the evidence obtained provides a reasonable basis for our findings and conclusions based on our audit objectives.

End Notes

[1] The OECD is an organization of 34 industrialized countries, operating by consensus, that fosters dialogue among members to discuss, develop, and refine economic and social policies and provides an arena for establishing multilateral agreements.

[2] They can take the form of "supplier credits," extended by the exporter, or "buyer credits," where the exporter's bank or financial institution lends to the buyer or to the buyer's bank.

[3] These are Ex-Im's definitions. Ex-Im and OECD officials noted that there are not consistent definitions for "short-term," "medium-term," and "long-term."

[4] Ex-Im's budget includes its program subsidy and its administrative expenses. Program subsidy refers to budgetary resources that must be allocated annually to reserve against any estimated costs to the government of Ex-Im's activities (such as due to defaults) not covered by fees and other payments, on a net present value basis. The fees charged by Ex-Im have covered its annual subsidy and administrative costs in recent years. Congress retains oversight of Ex-Im's budget by setting annual limits on Ex-Im's use of its funds for program subsidy and administrative expenses.

[5] Overseas investment loans (loans to help domestic firms invest abroad) and untied loans (loans extended to foreign governments or companies for the purpose of providing credit for strategic reasons) are offered by JBIC. Overseas untied loan insurance, which protects Japanese companies and banks from losses associated with providing untied loans, is provided by NEXI.

[6] Specifically, the remaining G-7 countries had the following shares: United States: 0.6 percent, Canada: 0.3 percent, France: 1.1 percent, Germany: 0.6 percent, Japan: 0.2 percent.

[7] We found that the data presented in Ex-Im's *Report to the U.S. Congress on Export Credit Competition and the Export-Import Bank of the United States, period January 2010 through December 2010* (Ex-Im 2010 Competitiveness Report) provide the best available estimate of the G-7 ECAs' medium- and long-term officially supported export credits. The amounts are estimated because some ECAs do not specifically report this information. Rather, they report on their total business, only a subset of which can be considered "officially supported" export credits. This makes it very difficult to obtain the information shown in figure 3 from ECA annual reports.

[8] The European Union is an economic and political partnership among 27 European countries. Austria, Belgium, Bulgaria, Cyprus, the Czech Republic, Denmark, Estonia, Finland, France, Germany, Greece, Hungary, Ireland, Italy, Latvia, Lithuania, Luxembourg, Malta, the Netherlands, Poland, Portugal, Romania, Slovakia, Slovenia, Spain, Sweden, and the United Kingdom are members.

[9] The Arrangement also governs the use of "tied aid"—aid conditioned on the purchase of goods and services from the donor country.

[10] The latest version of the Arrangement dates from September 2011. An important change was the introduction of new buyer risk (commercial) premium rates, which came into effect on September 1, 2011.

[11] Canada experienced a large increase in 2009, which is largely related to restructuring of the automotive sectors in Canada and the United States.

[12] As shown in figure 4, some of the European ECAs have interest make-up programs, which are designed to facilitate fixed-rate lending and provide an alternative to direct loans. However, according to Ex-Im and Treasury officials, because of the reliance of such programs on commercial banks as intermediaries and a lack of liquidity during the financial crisis, Ex-Im's direct loan product was more competitive.

[13] Ex-Im interprets the term "make available" as a target that the bank is expected to meet.

[14] In fiscal years 2002-2005, Ex-Im did not reach the goal, with its small business financing share ranging from 16.9 percent to 19.7 percent.

[15] In terms of total number of transactions, transactions involving small business directly account for the bulk of Ex-Im financing because they are on average much smaller in value than transactions that directly involve larger businesses. In 2010, about 88 percent of the total number of Ex-Im's transactions directly benefited small business and about 25 percent were made available to non-small business. (The percentages do not sum to 100 because some individual transactions could be used to directly benefit multiple parties, including both small and non-small businesses.)

[16] Ex-Im officials said they requested funding in fiscal year 2011 for expanding small business outreach efforts, but that funding was not included in their final budget.

[17] Ex-Im's financing of exports it identified as environmentally beneficial was 1.3 percent of its total financing from fiscal year 2003 through the first half of fiscal year 2010. Its financing of the more narrowly defined category of renewable energy and energy-efficient technologies would be much smaller than 1.3 percent of its total financing. We found that Ex-Im could improve its planning and use of resources in this area, although the difficulty of meeting these targets with existing resources remained to be seen. GAO, *Export-Import Bank: Reaching New Targets for Environmentally Beneficial Exports Presents Major Challenges for Bank*, GAO-10-682 (Washington, D.C.: July 14, 2010).

[18] Ex-Im has additional requirements. They include, for example, annual reporting requirements on its small business activities and the requirement to develop a program for providing

support with respect to the export of high technology items to countries making the transition to market-based economies.

[19] To be eligible for Ex-Im support, Ex-Im requires that certain transactions be shipped exclusively on U.S.-flagged vessels if the cargo is oceanborne. These transactions include (1) direct loans, regardless of the amount, and (2) guarantee transactions with either (a) a financed amount greater than $20 million or (b) a repayment period greater than 7 years.

[20] In 2002, Ex-Im's energy financing, specifically its financing for fossil fuel projects, was the subject of a lawsuit brought against the bank and the Overseas Private Investment Corporation by environmental nongovernmental organizations and four U.S. cities. *Friends of the Earth, Inc., et al. v. Spinelli, et al.* (Civ. No. 02-4106, N.D. Cal.) The lawsuit asserted that Ex-Im and the Overseas Private Investment Corporation (OPIC) provided assistance for fossil fuel projects that caused greenhouse gas emissions without complying with provisions of the National Environmental Policy Act requiring assessments of their projects' impacts on the U.S. environment resulting from their emissions. The lawsuit was settled in 2009 with Ex-Im agreeing to develop and implement a carbon policy for Ex-Im's financing; provide the Board of Directors with additional information about carbon dioxide emissions associated with potential fossil fuel transactions; and take a leadership role in consideration of climate change issues, promoting emissions mitigation measures within the Organisation for Economic Cooperation and Development and among export credit agencies.

[21] The enhanced due diligence process is an early review by Ex-Im's Board of highcarbon-intensity projects, such as coal-fired power plants, which includes a requirement for verifiable offsets to reduce the carbon dioxide intensity of projects in the highest category.

[22] For information on Ex-Im's economic impact assessment process, see GAO, *Export-Import Bank: Improvements Needed in Assessment of Economic Impact*, GAO-07-1071 (Washington, D.C.: Sept. 12, 2007).

[23] Specifically, congressional notification is required if the transaction is for the export of technology, fuel, equipment, materials, or goods or services to be used in the construction, alteration, operation, or maintenance of nuclear power, enrichment, reprocessing, research, or heavy water production facilities.

[24] Financing 85 percent of the total value of a transaction is considered full financing because of the provision under the OECD Arrangement that ECAs can finance only 85 percent of a transaction's value.

[25] Thus, the domestic content percentage of a transaction is calculated as a fraction of the total value of the transaction, including direct costs, indirect costs, and profit.

[26] For small businesses' short-term transactions, Ex-Im requires that the aggregate U.S. content of all products in an export transaction must be more than 50 percent. The amount of foreign content is calculated from the exporter's total direct and indirect costs, excluding profit. For non-small businesses, Ex-Im requires that each product in an export transaction have at least 50 percent U.S. content. In addition, the amount of foreign content is calculated from the exporter's direct cost only.

[27] Ex-Im makes exceptions to its domestic content requirement for tied aid, which has been used by Ex-Im four times in the last 10 years. According to Ex-Im officials, in addition to tied aid, Ex-Im allows raw materials that originated outside the United States to be considered 100 percent U.S. content when the raw material is significantly transformed (i.e., loses its identity) and constitutes a minimal (small) portion of the value of the end product.

[28] In 2007, the OECD Arrangement participants agreed to raise the proportion of local costs that may be officially supported in an export contract from 15 percent to 30 percent of the export contract value on a trial basis through the end of 2010. In 2008, Ex-Im increased its

maximum local cost support to 30 percent. In January 2011, the local cost provision was made permanent in the Arrangement text.

[29] Thus, for a transaction with an export value of $100, of which $10 was foreign content, Ex-Im would have financed $76.50 before 1987 ($90 x 0.85) and would finance $85 under its current policy.

[30] Congress requires Ex-Im to conduct an annual survey of exporters and lenders who have used Ex-Im's medium- and long-term programs in the prior calendar year to determine their experience using the bank's programs and to compare these programs with those of other ECAs. Ex-Im's most recent report, published in June 2011, covers the period January 1, 2010, through December 31, 2010.

[31] According to Ex-Im's charter, Congress directs Ex-Im to provide guarantees, insurance, and extensions of credit at rates and on terms and other conditions that are fully competitive with the government-supported rates and terms and other conditions available for the financing of exports of goods and services from the principal countries whose exporters compete with U.S. exporters.

[32] Concessionality refers to the percentage of financing that is a grant or grant equivalent.

[33] In the past, the OECD released an annual report containing aggregations of the data that ECAs reported on their export credit transactions. However, according to OECD officials, the last report issued was for 2005, and in recent years, their data collection mechanism has not allowed for sufficiently reliable reporting. The officials said they plan to begin releasing these data again in early 2012. They hoped this would coincide with the implementation of the new data reporting directive.

[34] Italy's ECA, SACE, operates a market window for some non-export credit activities. SACE officials emphasized that all of its export credit transactions fall under Arrangement terms. Germany's KfW IPEX-Bank, owned by KfW Bankengruppe (KfW), also operates a market window. KfW was criticized as having an unfair advantage because it had access to cheaper funding for export lending and project finance activities because of its state backing. In 2002, as part of a settlement with the European Commission, Germany agreed to separate KfW's commercial business from the rest of its activities, and in 2004, it began conducting much of its export credit and project finance activities through KfW IPEX-Bank. In 2008, KfW-IPEX-Bank became an independent legal entity.

[35] Although the financing is market-based, the ECAs delivering it have a government connection and can enjoy benefits associated with that status, such as tax exemptions. In addition, one concern has been that ECAs with market windows might use profits from the market transactions to subsidize their transactions under the Arrangement.

[36] Arrangement members are permitted, consistent with international obligations and the purpose of the Arrangement, to match financial terms and conditions offered by nonmembers.

[37] China has two official ECAs—China Ex-Im Bank and Sinosure. China Ex-Im Bank offers loans and loan guarantees; it also offers concessional loans that are comparable to what the OECD refers to as "official development assistance." Sinosure is an export credit insurer and offers programs covering short-, medium- and long-term export credit insurance as well as foreign investment insurance. China Development Bank, a Chinese policy bank, does not consider itself to be an official ECA, but has offered export credit financing. In some projects it finances, it stipulates that a certain amount of materials and equipment have to be sourced from China.

End Notes for Appendix I

[1] See GAO, *Export-Import Bank: Performance Standards for Small Business Assistance Are in Place but Ex-Im Is in the Early Stages of Measuring Their Effectiveness*, GAO-08-915 (Washington, D.C.: July 2008); *Export-Import Bank: Reaching New Targets for Environmentally Beneficial Exports Presents Major Challenges for Bank*, GAO-10-682 (Washington, D.C.: July 2010); and *Export-Import Bank: Improvements Needed in Assessment of Economic Impact*, GAO-07-1071 (Washington, D.C.: September 2007).

IDNEX

T